Vietnam Memoirs

Vietnam Memoirs

a passage to sorrow

J. Robert Falabella

NAVAL INSTITUTE PRESS
Annapolis, Maryland

Naval Institute Press
291 Wood Road
Annapolis, MD 21402-5043

First Naval Institute Press paperback edition 2010

Library of Congress Cataloging-in-Publication Data

Falabella, J. Robert, 1930–
Vietnam memoirs : a passage to sorrow / J. Robert Falabella.
    p. cm.
  Originally published: New York: Pageant Press International. c1971.
  ISBN 978-1-59114-255-3 (alk. paper)
  1. Vietnam War, 1961-1975—Personal narratives, American.
2. Vietnam War, 1961-1975—Chaplains—United States. 3. Falabella, J. Robert, 1930- I. Title.
  DS559.5.F35 2010
  959.704'37—dc22
  [B]
2010009802

Printed in the United States of America on acid-free paper

16 15 14 13 12 11 10   9 8 7 6 5 4 3 2
First printing

TO MY PARENTS
whose sacrifices taught me
the meaning of love.

Foreword

Vietnam Memoirs: A Passage to Sorrow is an account of an American's experiences and observations while serving with an infantry division in South Vietnam. The writer was beyond draft age, and so volunteered for a three year enlistment in the Army in order to serve the American troops in Vietnam. While aware of the positions of those speaking for and against American involvement in the war, the writer found himself concerned most directly with those fellow Americans who were actually serving in Vietnam in obedience to the call of their government. He felt a need to be with them, to give something of himself, for they were the ones who seemed to be forgotten in the bitter conflict that raged at home on the wisdom or foolishness of such American involvement. While in Vietnam for a year, which included the first Tet Offensive, the writer had many opportunities to be with various combat battalions in his capacity as a chaplain. Desiring to experience the hardships and strain of combat soldiers, so as to better appreciate the nature of their work, the author lived with them in the field and accompanied them on various missions. In the process of being with these troops for a year, alarming signs of inconsistency were observed in what was taking place, causing a reassessment of certain viewpoints formerly held by the author. In this account, we see a man who loves his country, and so is concerned over the implications of what he had observed.

Vietnam Memoirs

one

"**W**elcome to Bien Hoa, Vietnam," said the chief stewardess through the intercom. Her voice was quiet and calm with the kind of tone that could just as well be saying, "Welcome to Chicago," or "Welcome to Los Angeles." But throughout the massive jet there was little enthusiasm shown by the troops. Rather, there was an apprehensive silence which made the shrill shrieks of the Boeing jets all the more ear-shattering as they slowly moved the massive aircraft to its discharge point. No doubt it was a polite custom to so welcome a plane's passengers to their destination, and in more normal circumstances it would have been most appropriate. Here, however, to men in uniform entering an alien country where they would be regarded as a necessary evil to some of the residents and as outright enemies to others, such a "welcome" seemed painful.

The pilot's voice came over the intercom requesting all passengers to remain in their seats and announcing that a military liaison officer would board the plane and give further instructions. The jets gave one last plaintive cry and fell silent. The soldiers within the aircraft were motionless. They seemed to be clinging tenaciously to that silence as if it were the last vestige of a womb before their abrupt entrance into a world and a life they would rather not enter.

The liaison officer boarded the plane and officially informed us that we were now officially in South Vietnam. We were told to sign a statement that we had not brought into the country any weapons. This seemed on the surface to be rather ironic. The officer then directed us to leave the plane and go immediately to a hangar-like area for further instructions.

Slowly the soldiers lifted their now seemingly heavy bodies from the comfort and apparent protection of their luxurious

1

seating accommodations—the last bit of comfortable living that many of them would enjoy for quite some time—and started to file out from the plane. What kind of men made up this flight? Wedding bands revealed some as married but by far the majority were single young men in their late teens or early twenties. Their eyes, however, did not seem to register on the present. They were, perhaps, too intent on seeing the past—their homes, their sweethearts, and the good life.

As the soldiers filed past the stewardesses, some of the men managed to say "Thank you," while others said nothing—so engrossed were they, no doubt, with their own memories or the sudden awareness as to where they really were. I noticed that the stewardesses at this time no longer were the epitome of zestfulness. The smile on their lovely faces seemed as though threatening tears at any moment. Just hours earlier these young girls were laughing and joking with the men. Now the plane was back on earth and there was no more laughter. Their passengers were in Vietnam. And as the troops filed past these stewardesses, who could well have been their sisters or wives, the tear-filled eyes of those young girls revealed, I believe, what they were thinking at that moment: "How many of these young boys, filled with such exuberance for life, would make that return flight a year from now?"

As we approached the large hangar-like structure where we were to assemble for further instructions, a tremendous roar of approval came up from that area where the troops who had completed their tour in Vietnam waited to board the plane we had just left. I recall the wild whistling, laughter, and vociferous comments such as, "Good luck"; "Hope you make it"; "It's a long year, Buddy"; "You poor sons of . . . ," and so on.

I wondered how we must look to them. The thought occurred to me that if we survived the year in Vietnam we also would have the opportunity of welcoming our replacements and then we would see how we once had looked on our arrival. We would have the similar thrill of seeing those men who would be replacing us—men who presently were either in some school or working at some job and apprehensively awaiting the Damoclean sword of the draft. We found our hearts beating faster at the thought of the day when "going home" would be a reality. How acutely anxious we were becoming for it already. Yet as much as we wanted to board the plane and return to the States with those howling, ecstatically excited GI's, we knew we really did not belong—not yet. We would have to earn that place in the plane. For some, that return trip home would cost them everything they possessed.

A GI officer with a bull horn directed us to place our baggage into a large trailer truck. We then were told to board the bus which would transport us to the replacement center in Long Binh—a sprawling supply center and headquarters area for the Americans. The ride in the bus was quiet. No one had much to say. The windows had metal screens over them for the purpose, I was told, of preventing grenades from being thrown inside. I recall how dirty the streets and hovels were that we passed and easily imagined some one shooting at us along such narrow streets. As it happened, we were not shot at.

All of us were confused. Wasn't this Vietnam? Wasn't a war going on here? There certainly was a war going on but only experience would teach us just what kind of a war it was. Only personal experience in the combat zones would reveal just how low the danger factor actually was in Long Binh or such other areas as Saigon, Tan Son Nhut or Cam Ranh Bay. This is not to say a person could not get killed in such places, but compared to the combat zones the chances were slight. I would gradually realize there was little equity in combat troops receiving the same "extra combat pay' as those stationed in such relatively safe areas. This extra combat pay was sixty-five dollars extra a month, provided you were in a combat zone. All Vietnam was so termed but anyone with experience could see no parallel between the Boi Loi Woods and Tan Son Nhut, much less Cam Ranh Bay. In my account, the use of the term "combat zone" is taken to mean those areas where the troops are not only dressed in battle gear, but are in areas where combat with the enemy is most likely and where the living conditions are generally "field," with all that that implies to any "grunt" or "crunchy." This will become clearer in the following pages.

When we arrived at the replacement center, there was a large "Welcome" sign to greet us. The first thing we did there that made separation from our homeland seem complete was to turn in our American currency and receive its equivalent in military scrip. We were directed to rent the necessary bedclothes at the administration building and then go to our appointed barracks to await further instructions.

Locating my assigned barracks, I went in and found an empty bunk. The barracks were long wooden structures with coarse cement floors. Some Vietnamese women were inside sweeping the floor with a makeshift broom. I was surprised at how small the women were. Some of the women appeared young. The smile of the older women presented a pathetic picture. You could see that a number of their teeth were missing and those that remained were heavily stained from chewing red betel nut. I was told this nut had some anesthetizing properties which aided in relieving toothaches.

Within the barracks were also some GI's who had completed their tour and were waiting for their flight back to the States. One of them was pleasant with the Vietnamese women; the other acted crudely and even with hostility when one of the women tried to be friendly. I would find that this is about how things would be after a year. Some Americans would accept the Vietnamese and others would loathe them. It was no doubt mutual with the Vietnamese.

An instruction came over the loudspeaker that all arrivals should attend the orientation briefing, which turned out to be a boring repeat performance of what we heard from our Vietnam orientation back in the States. Slides were shown of Vietnam as though we were coming as tourists. The lecturer again exhorted us to be good ambassadors. If the lecturer was as condescending to the Vietnamese as he was to us then he certainly was not practicing what he preached. The latter observation would have many parallels during my year in Vietnam and offer the basis for an etiological explanation of the serious problems within America itself.

As an arrival, you were to remain in the replacement compound until your actual assignment came down from higher headquarters. The waiting period was a day or two. I was to wait, however, four days before finally receiving some inkling of my assignment. A jeep came and took me to the headquarters building of USARV where I was briefed by the USARV chaplain who reminded me that there would be a lot of work to do and that I should not forget that I was a chaplain and so conduct myself. In asking what he meant by that statement I was told that a chaplain should not carry any weapons. This advice did not square with what I understood to be the Army regulation which simply stated that a chaplain would not be required to carry a weapon. This was a fair and reasonable statement, leaving it up to the conscience of the chaplain to make the final decision. Having had no experience of combat conditions in the field, I went along with the biased and unreasonable statements of the USARV chaplain and naively believed (until Tet) that not carrying a weapon was fitting in my circumstances and undoubtedly a brave thing to do. Actual experience later completely reversed this evaluation. How I arrived at that conclusion will be explained below. Suffice it for now to say that I was at that time in awe of what I thought was a realistic and sagacious senior chaplain. In time I would find out he no more knew what the real situation was "out there" in the hedgerows, rice paddies, plantation fields, and woods than most other high-ranking officers with their immaculately clean uniforms, shiny boots and air conditioned offices. Like so many senior officers and visiting VIPs from Congress, what he knew came from "quickie" visits to safe areas. None of those VIPs ever lived in the field with the troops who were doing the actual fighting.

They no more knew the real situation than did those pseudo-intellectuals in the States. In time I was to come to a shocking awareness of how poorly informed the decision makers really were. I recall hearing a general speak over the Armed Forces radio about an incident I was in. His assessment of that situation was quite optimistic. Having been there, I knew that was not the case—the significance of the enemy action was underestimated. The general's description was, to say the least, a magnificent expression of wishful thinking.

Another incident I recall was a brigade commander who was cursing over the intercom at some troops of a battalion who were moving slowly on the ground. This brigade commander was flying comfortably above in a nice cool helicopter. His uniform was as clean and spotless as his language was shoddy and foul. He could not understand why the troops were moving so slowly. What he said on that intercom was gross, surpassed only by his ignorance of the terrain the troops were in. From a helicopter the looks of the terrain far below can be deceptive. In fact the troops were trying to move through several feet of stinking slime at the hottest time of the day with full battle gear after having been continuously on the move for many hours. If the brigade commander had been on the ground, he never would have said the things he did nor would his viewpoint have been so one-sided. If there could be such ignorance even at this level of command, what must be the ignorance of those at still higher levels who are not even near the field of operations? Could one be surprised then at the policies coming from Washington when there was such ignorance even at these levels? As the months passed in Vietnam, I found myself becoming more and more disillusioned with the competency of the American military and political leadership. Hard experience would unmask the myth of their purported efficiency and resourcefulness. However, at the time of my briefing, I was quite inexperienced about the general situation.

Having had my interview with the USARV chaplain, I was returned to the replacement station and a day later received my assignment to the 25th Infantry Division, which had its base in the Cu Chi area, about a half-hour's drive from Saigon. On arrival at Cu Chi, I was met by a chaplain who directed me to in-processing. Once that was completed, I was shown the Support Command area where I was to take up my duties as an assistant chaplain. Actually I was there in that capacity for only about six weeks when I was asked to assume the duties of battalion chaplain for infantry troops. While with Support Command, however, there were some valuable experiences which served as a preparation for what was to be a demanding year.

The Support Command chaplain was affable. He introduced me to my duties, one of which was to visit the 25th Medical Detachment wards which were in five quonset buildings. The patients there were not considered sufficiently ill to be cared for at the 12th Evacuation Hospital, a quarter of a mile away. Although I made myself available to the patients for counseling, I found that most of my time in the wards was spent simply listening to the patients enumerate the things they would be doing once they returned to the States. I also discovered that apart from the religious functions on Sunday, there was little demand by the patients for religious ministrations.

The Support Command chaplain also had me assist him in orientations for the new arrivals. The format consisted of an introduction of ourselves as their chaplains and a description of the religious services on Sunday. We urged the troops to write home often, but suggested they refrain from telling the family how miserable they might feel since the people back home were suffering enough anguish simply being separated from them. Further, we advised the new troops not to relate in their letters gruesome "war stories" they might have heard since this would simply augment their families' fears. The support troops were reminded to think positively, do their job and keep alert. They were invited to come to our office any time they wished. We then released them and seldom saw them again.

Another duty was visiting the morgue. Any troops of my religious affiliation who were killed were to receive a certain religious administration if possible. The identification tag of the deceased contained an entry for this religious service. The people in charge of Graves Registration were usually careful to see to it that a Catholic chaplain was called. Generally the deceased had been dead for quite some time before a priest could be present. Nonetheless, a conditional administration was given and it was hoped by the Army that subsequent word of this might offer some measure of comfort to the bereaved parents or wife.

Being called to the morgue was always grim. But what was very shocking were the many cases of those who were killed accidentally by our own forces. For instance on one call to the morgue I was told that the bodies just brought in were killed by a short round from our own mortars. Another time a lieutenant was blown up when he attempted to dismantle a "dud" rocket. The great tragedy in this incident was that the lieutenant was conducting a class at the time and had most of his class around him. The number of Americans killed and maimed because of carelessness on the part of American troops would be shocking if a careful study were made. Later I will mention similar incidents which were costly in the loss of men and matériel.

I especially recall when I arrived at Cu Chi how crude the morgue facilities were and how severe was the odor of death. The bodies were tagged and prepared to be sent for embalming elsewhere in Vietnam. Being called to the morgue and waiting for the black sack to be zippered down was always a terrible ordeal. Especially difficult was viewing these young boys and these young men so violently torn from life. I often would think of the deep affliction that would befall their loved ones on receiving the news of their deaths. Little did I realize then that I would someday, as death notification officer in the States, come to know the final chapter of such tragic stories begun here in Vietnam.

two

Since I thought that my job with Support Command would be for the duration of my stay in Vietnam, I began the necessary adjustment to the living conditions of Cu Chi. Coming from the States and never having known anything but indoor plumbing, hot water, clean sheets and a soft bed, Cu Chi was an uncomfortable environment. Little did I realize then how fortunate I was to be assigned a job which kept me in Cu Chi. Later on I would find out how wonderful the living conditions there were compared to "field existence." At this time I only knew of modern city living in the States and so the standards in Cu Chi were crude and distasteful. Outdoor latrines were bad enough but to have no privacy inside them was obnoxious. I had a great deal to learn. My mind could tell me that such a condition was understandable given the situation we were in but my overly sensitive nature constantly rebelled at such primitive conditions. Nor have I totally changed in this matter to this day, even after further experiences which made the living conditions at Cu Chi seem almost palatial.

The water you washed with was tepid to cool and you were warned not to drink it, such were its impurities. The cleaning of one's uniform was done by the Vietnamese, evidently in buffalo water. Once your clothes received that first cleaning, you would be living with a peculiarly rank odor in your clothes for the rest of your tour in Vietnam. After a while, you could almost get used to it but the odor of the burning "honey pots" (defecated matter) giving forth their dank sickening odors was always present to nauseate you. Dirt, dust, heat, stench—this was Cu Chi. I did not, however, appreciate how fortunate I was being there. To my inexperienced self, nothing could be worse than this place. I was to find out there certainly was.

Just as I was becoming acquainted with my new job, the division chaplain came to my office one morning and asked how I felt about taking on the chaplain's slot in a mechanized infantry battalion. The chaplain there was finishing his tour and would be leaving in less than two weeks. The problem was that his replacement would be several weeks late. As this job dealt with combat troops, the division chaplain considered that priority should be given them. He did not relish their not having their own chaplain even for a short period of time. This new assignment would be difficult since, beside this mechanized battalion, I would as the Catholic chaplain also have to cover two other straight infantry battalions: the 1st and 2nd of the 27th Wolf-hounds. The job would entail going out to the field each week for five days or so, during which I would have to find a way of reaching those three battalions as best I could and returning to Cu Chi on Saturday to check the 12th Evacuation Hospital for the wounded men from those battalions. On Sunday there would be three morning services to be conducted in Cu Chi before going out in the afternoon to begin another week in the field with the combat troops.

My first reaction was not enthusiastic. Cu Chi was now even comfortable to me. I had adapted to its primitive way of life and, having briefly visited the field one afternoon for a couple of hours to hold a service, I realized how far superior Cu Chi was in living conditions. Besides, Cu Chi was a safe haven at this time. I was told that it had been many months since Cu Chi was even mortared. Life in Cu Chi, at least for the present, was rather secure. To rationalize my not accepting this offer by the division chaplain to work with combat troops, I further reminded myself of the time I had been spending in learning the Vietnamese language: first back in the States where I spent hours listening to tapes and now in Cu Chi where I was attending a class conducted by charming Vietnamese. My plans were to work with the civil-affairs groups and ultimately conduct a religious service in the Vietnamese language, which I thought would be a further token of American good will. I had also been teaching a Vietnamese priest how to say the service in English and he was reciprocating by showing me how to do the same in Vietnamese.

The thought that my plans to be involved in civil affairs would have to be shelved, after I had gotten myself used to the idea that such would be a meaningful contribution to the American effort, was far from attractive. Making the rounds in the medical-detachment infirmary did not take long, and the Support troops evidently found no need for a Catholic chaplain except for the Sunday service. I wanted more to do, and the civil-affairs section looked like the area where I could be of greater service. With this attitude, I was unenthusiastic about the suggestion of the division chaplain that I leave this job and go off to a new way of living and an entirely different routine of operations. If I had arrived at Cu Chi and was given a combat chaplain's job—fine, but to be settled down in an entirely different role and then be uprooted—this was much like a similar situation when I was uprooted from the familiar life of a Stateside Army training area to the strangeness of life in this foreign country.

While my feelings were strong, my mind told me that my role as a chaplain was primarily one of service to others and not to myself. What I liked was not the point; rather where I was most needed. My mind prevailed over my feelings and I told the division chaplain I would accept the new job. Within a week, I would be going out to the field.

It was with grim reluctance that I moved my quarters from Support Command to the battalion area of the 5th Mechanized Battalion. I was just getting used to my quarters at the Support area. I had sandbagged around the tent in which I lived. I was coming to know people in the area. The enlisted men's club for the medic personnel was just a few feet away, and I used to like to hear a combo of medics who played there at night. One song they played and sang with real soul was the "House of the Rising Sun." It was a plaintive song which seemed to fit the environment we were in—being away from home; hearing stories of the fire fights; seeing wounded people; making periodic visits to the morgue. Now I would have to leave the place where I was living. After coming to accept this "new life," I found myself about to make another move into what was strange and unknown to me.

My gear was packed into the jeep and I was taken to another section of Cu Chi—the compound of the 5th Mech. I had driven by that area many times, as well as passed the Wolfhound compounds. I always felt uncomfortable when going by them. "That's where the combat troops are," the jeep driver would tell me. "Not too many people in those compounds, though, since the battalions are out in the field looking for the enemy. They do a lot of fighting and also get killed." The thought of men being killed, the odor of the "honey pots," the dirt, the dust and the heat—all made the situation oppressive. It seemed I was being drawn closer to the real thing; all that goes into the ugliness of violence, of combat, of war. I did not know by experience what these things were— only what I read and saw in pictures. Now I was beginning to feel a presence or awareness of something starkly forbidding, and I suspected it would be far worse than I ever imagined.

The outgoing chaplain of the 5th Mech was on hand to greet me when I arrived. He was a pleasant gentleman who had distinguished himself in his year of service in Vietnam. I noticed on his desk the set of ribbons he would be wearing back to the States. There was a bronze star for heroism and a purple heart. All he ever seemed to say was how great his "Bobcats" were— the men of the 5th Mech. This man was proud of his troops. His enthusiasm for the Mech was astounding. "If you're going to be a cat, be a Bobcat," he would say over and over again. I noticed, however, a tenseness in his neck and a tautness about his lips that indicated he had endured some hard times—and he could not disguise it with his attempts at laughter and jovial banter.

Everywhere I went with this chaplain I was reminded by those I met that they were going to miss him, that he was the greatest in their book and that they certainly would not want to be the one trying to replace him. I would find that this was a natural reaction among the troops if they liked their chaplain. They were used to him. They knew him and he knew them. Now he was leaving and a stranger was taking his place. There would be little warmth of recognition on the part of the troops until the new man proved himself. I realized this and accepted the cool reserve of the troops stoically.

three

My predecessor had departed. In a few weeks the young soldier who was his assistant would also be going home. Before me was a new routine of operations I had to learn almost immediately. There were religious services on Sundays at Cu Chi and then off to the field for a week of searching after the various battalions. What would it be like out there? How would I go about the routine? It was suggested that as soon as I got out to the field headquarters, I should locate the CP (Command Post), pay my respects to the battalion commander and request permission for a time to hold services. My mission was to try and reach three battalions each week. Since the troops are normally away from the field camp during the day, it would not be until the evening that I could hold services. This would also mean I would have to sleep out with the troops in the field, since there would be no transportation out of that area until sometime the next morning. I would have to bring camping gear along with me. Again, I found myself in a strange situation—an unknown. Further, I counted heavily on the chaplain's assistant to drive me around Cu Chi for the services, since most of Cu Chi was relatively unknown to me. But shortly this assistant would also be going back home, so I knew I had to learn as much as possible of what had to be done in Cu Chi.

I was told a new assistant would be sent to me, but what I needed then was not someone new. I was new enough. I realized I was on my own and that I was looking for someone to lean on, but there was no one. It was my job and responsibility and I had to find the strength to face up to it.

The first thing I did was acquaint myself with the broken-down jeep that was allotted the chaplain. I then acquired my military license to drive the jeep legally and found out where I was to go to pump gas for the jeep when needed. My original thought was to purchase a motorcycle and use that for my needs inside and outside Cu Chi, but I was informed that was forbidden because of the hazards of the roads. So I had to settle for the jeep. I felt much better now about my situation. If I did not have an assistant, I'd make do. The job would get done. As it turned out, when the assistant left it was several weeks before his replacement arrived. By that time, I was on to the routine and no longer felt any need for an assistant. My reaction to the knock on my office door early one morning in December was almost belligerent when the young man announced he was the chaplain's new assistant. Some weeks ago when I knew nothing, I wanted someone. I needed someone. I had to go through the experience of having no assistance and painfully adjusted myself. Now an assistant came whom I would have to take the time to train. As will be seen, this new assistant turned out to be remarkably efficient and became a wonderful friend who began to think so closely along my channel that even when I was not present to request him to do certain things, he instinctively did them. To this day, I consider myself fortunate in having Wally Nelson as my assistant while I was with the 5th Mech.

It would be, however, several weeks before Wally would come on the scene and it was during that period that I began to become trained to a whole new concept of a chaplain's work, a combat chaplain. The role of such a chaplain is to be closely associated with combat troops in the field, sleeping as they do, eating their food and sharing at times the hazardous moments of their lives.

This type of living is far removed from Cu Chi, just as Cu Chi is far removed from the high living conditions and great security of Cam Ranh Bay, Tan Son Nhut or Saigon. It is out in the field with the combat troops that one comes to the end of the line. It is here that you find the *raison d'etre* of every other aspect of the military structure. It is here that one comes to the

15

moment of truth; it is here that the disgusting horror of hostile confrontation takes place. It is at this point that you suddenly realize that combat and war are not like anything you have read about or imagined. It is here you realize that combat is far from a game as you have known games to be, and that the only tragedy worse than war is the treatment of it as though it were a game. Saying that one knows this and experiencing it are far from the same thing. It would take more than a brief visit to the field to come to this awareness. It would take almost a year of close living with combat troops to have this awareness take hold of the very depths of my being.

four

remember vividly my first extended trip to the field. The gear consisted of my religious service kit, a poncholiner and blanket, a poncho and mosquito net, an air mattress, a hip shovel, two canteens of water, a safety razor, shaving cream, and a small steel mirror. In time, the shaving cream and mirror would no longer be among the items for I soon accustomed myself to shaving in the dark by simply dabbing a few drops of water at a time on my face and listening for the scraping sound to inform me something was happening. After a while I could almost imagine my face before a mirror and shaved as though it were really there.

Now that I was packed, the next step was to get out to the field. To do that there were different options available. At times (and this was generally the case before Tet) you would go to "Row Bravo," a supply point where the Chinooks would load on the ammunition and other supplies, as well as the chow, water, and mail. Troops would also be taken out on these runs. If you went by Chinook, it usually meant the roads were not usable, or there were no roads and the terrain was impassable for vehicles. There was usually a morning and afternoon supply available for the battalion's use. When you could board the Chinook depended on the supply officers on duty at Row Bravo. I found them to be helpful and most of the time they would get me on the first run. If I did not take the morning supply, there would be one in the afternoon leaving any time between 1300 and 1600 hours. Chinooks would be seen coming in and going out continuously since there were other battalions to be supplied besides the ones I covered.

Waiting in the sun two, three, or more hours at Row Bravo was torturous. Also, the dust swirling about by the rotor blades at near gale force every time a Chinook came in or took off caked a layer of grime all over you. It was difficult to even speak while waiting under these conditions. In any event, no one there—and this would be the supply personnel and the troops on their way back to the field——was in a mood for conversation. The combat troops might have come into Cu Chi for dental work or administrative reasons. Once away from combat, they were not overly anxious about returning. The comparative safety of Cu Chi intensified the feeling of danger when one returned to the field. There was a price, of course, a trooper would have to pay if he did come into Cu Chi, and that was the harassment of having his boots polished and all insignia properly sewn on his uniform before he was allowed to visit the PX, which was the big attraction. In some ways the PX was a vestige of the "world" they left back in the States. In the PX, there were radios, hi-fi equipment, clothes, magazines, canned foods, candy, cameras—all sorts of things to get your mind off where you were. There in the PX you could do for a few moments what thousands of Americans were doing back home in the States (or the "world" as the troops called it)—namely, buying things—even if you didn't need them. It was the great American way—coming out of a store with a bag filled with goodies.

So the troops waiting to return to the field would have mixed emotions. There would not be that excessive harassment of spit shine boots out in the field, but then there would be the harassment of "Charlies."

The word finally was given by the supply officer that the next incoming Chinook would be ours and to board it immediately on touch down. All then would run on the double to the pick-up point. Usually large thermos containers of food were shoved on board first, along with the mail and combat equipment. As I left the bright glare of the sun and entered into the strange dim chasm of the Chinook's belly, the screeching, shrieking motors pounded my eardrums and I felt dizzy. I would soon become accustomed to that cacophony. The troops and I sat across from one another. There were no safety belts used. If the Chinook ever crashed—with all those metal containers, machine gun replacements, and heavily-equipped troops, it was hard to conceive anybody escaping injury. Fortunately in our sector there were no Chinook crashes, except one that occurred just outside the perimeter of Cu Chi, while returning from the field. The hydraulic system failed and all sixteen aboard were killed.

With a thunderous groan our Chinook rose from the ground. We were airborne. This was my first Chinook ride. There would be many more before I would leave Vietnam. As the Chinook increased its altitude, more and more of the Cu Chi base camp unfolded before my eyes. The fringe of the camp was surrounded by several rows of barbed wire, with defensive bunkers and observation towers arranged at intervals behind the inner wire. A continuous road circled the camp just behind the towers and bunkers. I felt as if I were looking down upon a frontier outpost protecting itself from the hostile environment.

The inner part of the camp contained numerous rectangular-shaped, wooden barracks made of wood with corrugated metal roofs that glittered in the afternoon sun. Here and there were small islands of field command tents, as well as the long quonset structures that comprised the medical facilities. The small air field stood out conspicuously with its Huey Cobra gunships, as did the various helicopter pads, among which was Row Bravo. Flitting tongues of black smoke issuing from various honey pots seemed to mar the overall view with dark discolorations.

We were now high enough to see the surrounding area of the Cu Chi base camp. One side looked toward the village of Cu Chi less than half a mile away. Between this village and our division base camp was a settlement which only recently came into being, Bac Ha 1. Its thirty or so shanty tin structures were hurriedly put together when the division base camp came into being. Most of the people in Bac Ha 1 were residents of Saigon who came out to this area to open up their little shops, which included bars and brothels. GI's would bring their trucks and jeeps to Bac Ha and have the Viets wash them. This was easier than doing it themselves. Laundry concessions also catered to GI needs.

Soon the division base camp, Cu Chi village, and the Bac Ha settlement disappeared from view. From my vantage point in the Chinook, the panorama of the Vietnamese terrain was before my eyes. I was fascinated by the verdurous and lush fields. It was hard to believe a war was going on—everything appeared so peaceful and still: a multigreen and silvery quilt of vegetable gardens, hedgerows, and rice paddies basking in the bright sun.

The flight to the 2nd of the 27th Wolfhounds' area of operation took only about twenty minutes. The Chinook began its swift descent. The picture-card look soon gave way to movement as trees, bushes, and rice shoots started to dance—first ever so gently, but as the Chinook approached closer to the ground, the dance become wilder and wilder and then just as suddenly all but ended as the Chinook landed and discharged its cargo.

As I left the Chinook I did not know where to go, so I followed behind the troops. This was fine until we entered a wooded area and the troops began moving in different directions. I called in desperation to one of the GI's lest I be left all alone and asked for directions to the CP (Command Post). He told me to follow him and after some walking pointed to another little trail which would take me there. I thanked him and soon came upon an area with ponchos set up as tents, some mortar emplacements, and scattered supply boxes. I asked a husky looking GI where the Commanding Officer was and was directed to a small hut further up the path. I put down my burdensome gear and went looking for the place. As I made a turn around the trail I came upon the hut. Coming out was a thin, serious-looking gentleman who turned out to be the battalion commander. I reported to him, introduced myself as the new Catholic chaplain and requested permission to hold religious services. The CO said that would be fine, but the troops were not back yet from a mission and he suggested I hold my service at 1900 hours that evening. I thanked him and returned to where I had left my gear. It was now about 1600 hours. I asked the same husky GI where the various companies were set up so that I could visit those areas and put up a sign reminding the troops on their return that Catholic services would be held in the Headquarters Company area. The GI, whose name was Bob, gave me a general direction and with that I set off. The trail was thick and I wondered if a VC would jump out at me. As this was my first experience in the field, I naturally expected the worse.

Soon I came upon a clearing where Company A was set up. I spoke a while with a couple of the GI's there and then went to the mess area and asked for a paper plate, on which I printed "Catholic Services, HQS Company Area, 1900 hrs." I taped the paper plate on a large thermos jug so that as the troops passed by those concerned would get the message. I went through this same routine with B, C, and D Companies. It was when I was at D Company that the troops returned. Their faces showed they were tired and hungry. The sergeant of D Company invited me to eat with them, but as the troops lined up for chow it started to pour rain. I can still see one of the GI's standing slightly bent forward, his rifle slung over his shoulder, with his right hand holding a paper plate filled with food. His face showed great fatigue. He was staring at the plate, which had potatoes, beans, gravy, meat, and cake along with some salad all thrown together. The rain was now pouring and was dripping off his helmet, nose, and chin onto the soaked plate. It was such a gloomy looking figure I saw—a person who had just gone through a long hot day; sweated it out as the point man (the lead man in a search operation); looked forward to the moment when he would be back in the company area to enjoy a hot meal and, at the last moment, a downpour came and his meal was rapidly looking like mush, with the paper plate beginning to give way at the extremities. He tried to eat but the food was now sliding off the drooping plate. Then it happened. The plate totally collapsed depositing his dinner on the muddy ground. He let go in desperation with a one word expletive and walked away with his head down, too disgusted to even go back and get more food from the soggy mess line. It had been a miserable day for him and this topped it off. All that poor GI needed now was to find out that his squad would be the one appointed this night to go out on ambush. Tired, hungry, wet, and with little prospect of things getting better, the GI would go to his squad area and try to find some protection from the rain. With his luck, I wouldn't bet on it.

It was now becoming dark. I left D Company and returned to the HQS area to prepare for the services. The rain began to slacken off and finally stopped. I started to set up my Mass kit. I chose a spot right in the middle of HQS Company. The GI, Bob, came over to help me. A couple of ammunition boxes were put together for the altar. I put on my white vestments. A few of the GI's of HQS Company came over and sat on the damp ground. I spoke to them about the weather and the day's doings while anxiously looking about to see if anybody else would be there. It was just about dark now, and I could not expect to see any of the troops from the other companies walking through the dark trail to make the services. It dawned on me that the battalion commander had made a mistake in suggesting this time. This was my first lesson as a troop chaplain: you suggest the time to the commanding officer. Experience would show that they have other things on their minds, and that most of them are not concerned about what you came there for.

A few drops of rain began to fall on my face as I started the service. There I was, tired and still wet from the earlier downpour. Now with Mass about to begin and these weary, soaked GI's there to give worship to God, it was beginning to rain! In exasperation rather than with any irreverence, I prayed, "Father, can't you see how tired these boys are? How wet? They couldn't even get a hot meal tonight because of the rain. Now they are here at Mass to pray to you and it's starting to rain again. What kind of a Father are you? Are you going to let it rain at Mass after all they have been through today?" I then returned to the prayers of the Mass which were said in almost complete darkness. That was my first Mass in the field with this battalion. It was memorable, perhaps because the rain did stop for the remainder of the service.

At the end of the Mass, the GI's thanked me and disappeared into the darkness. Bob helped me put the service gear away. A lieutenant who was nearby asked if I was set up for the night. As it was, I did nothing to prepare a place for myself. I had forgotten all about it. I was told another lieutenant had gone to Cu Chi in the afternoon and would not be back until the morning. It was suggested I use his poncho-tent for the night. I was grateful.

With a shelter over me, I rested on the ground wrapped up in my poncho-liner. I went over what I had done that day. What did I learn? What were my mistakes? What routine would I have to work up so that I would not inconvenience some GI, like that young lieutenant who gave me his own place to sleep in on the pretext it was someone else's? The rain was again falling heavily. I thought of those GI's somewhere out there on ambush—cold and wet. I thought of that young lieutenant who gave me his place. I saw those tired faces of D Company. Somehow, the discomfort of the physical surroundings did not seem so formidable any longer.

Apparently the heavy rains kept the enemy mortar teams out of action. We had a quiet night in the field. Usually it was in the night that the enemy did his thing, such as planting mines, setting booby traps, and mortaring the battalion area. The saying was that the day belonged to our side but the night belonged to "Charlie." Just why the name "Charlie" was given the enemy probably has as many answers as there are people with imagination. A demeaning term, "gooks," was also used in bitterness to describe an enemy who seemed to thrive in fighting in slimy muck. While the term "Charlie" was most commonly heard, the more respectful "Charles" or even "Sir Charles" would be used by our troops when the enemy worked a particularly successful action against them. I was to find that the terms used by our troops in describing the enemy often was an indicator of their recent record against him as well as of the state of their morale.

It was about the middle of the morning before the supply Chinook finally arrived and I was able to return to Cu Chi. There I was told the good news that the 1st of the 27th Wolfhounds had come in for a three-day rest. Before the first Tet Offensive of the enemy, the battalions would normally go out to the field for a couple of weeks and then return to the base camp to wash up, take some training exercises, be entertained, visit the PX, and get away generally from the strain of field living. This also was a welcome opportunity to hold religious services inside a chapel building, which would afford the troops such comforts as chairs to sit upon and a roof to protect them from the sun or rain.

Not all battalion areas in Cu Chi had a chapel building, however, and I would find myself having to use a mess hall or, as in the case with the 1st of the 27th Wolfhounds, the enlisted men's club, which reeked of stale beer and cigar smoke from the party and "show" of the night before.

The entertainment of the troops varied from sensible and realistic to unseemly and even cruel. By sensible, I mean wholesome distractions from the tense scene that is combat and field living. Realistic entertainment takes into consideration the restricted environment the men are in, and so does nothing intentionally to stir up basic drives, in many cases already at a bursting point, and which are best left alone under the circumstances. What I mean by unseemly and cruel were those forms of entertainment such as "stag movies" which were nothing more than a perverted commercialism of sexual activity. This could hardly be refreshing and uplifting to troops who have been forced to live with the violent disorder and sordidness of combat. The troops would hoot and howl, and being normal would become sexually stimulated. The tragedy, however, was that they had no way of naturally releasing these aroused energies, and found themselves later in deep depression through the now intensified awareness of where they were, far from their homes, wives, and girl friends. Whoever was in charge of such matters either had a warped sense of humor or was grossly ignorant of what pressures of combat do to the sexual drives of men. That is not to say such ignorance, affected or otherwise, did not pay off. As often happens, there would be those who would make a fortune in presenting this kind of "distraction" to the GI's. But such unreasonable and ill-placed entertainment seemed to me sadistically cruel and deceptive, for it would leave the troops ultimately in a persistent hangover of depressing frustration. Certainly this was unworthy of people who claimed to be concerned about the well-being and morale of the troops.

I mentioned above that some of these shows were sponsored by the battalions. This meant that the financing of such shows came from the profits made from the sale of cold beer and soda to the troops in the field. One becomes intensely hot and thirsty out there, so something refreshingly cold is worth its weight in gold and is a sure seller. But what happens if you do not have the money to buy this cool refreshment? Well, then you had better borrow the scrip from someone or settle for the tepid-to-hot water in your canteen.

Somehow it never seemed right to me that a man who was thousands of miles from home, in a country he did not choose to be in, living in hardship and facing daily the risk of death, should have to relieve the discomfort of his thirst with his own money, if he was fortunate enough to have any.

It seemed to me that the combat troops I had known almost always appeared to get the "leftovers" rather than the "firsts." I recall troops in the field going around with rotted boots because the jungle boot was supposed to be scarce. Yet I also recall the noncombat troops such as people in administration with several pairs of such boots. The same seemed to be true of clothes, food, and anything else of value. The people who did the fighting were the lowest, last, and least. One thing they usually did get, however, was ammunition. No one else was especially interested in that. Some noncombatants, however, were interested in war trophies and would seek out combat troops to purchase a captured pistol or knife. Such a person would need this trophy to make his war stories more authentic. Beware of people who sport war trophies. The chances are they bought it from someone who really saw the action and wants nothing better than to forget the whole grim experience.

five

Several weeks had passed and I was feeling more at home in my new surroundings. I was growing better acquainted with field living. The routine of chasing after the battalions was becoming more and more of a challenge. What surprised me in my visits thus far to the field was that I had not as yet been on the receiving end of a mortar attack. On the evening of November 15th while in Cu Chi I had my first such experience.

There were some medics talking with me in my office quarters. A crunching sound was heard, metallic and sharp. Cu Chi was being hit with mortars for the first time in six months. Again and again the metallic earth-crunching sounds reached us. Mortars were definitely falling on the Bobcat battalion area. The troops I was conversing with had been in Vietnam for over ten months. They knew the difference between "incoming" and "outgoing." They fell to the floor and told me to do the same. With the kind of naive ignorance so prevalent among most people in matters of war, I was slow to agree with them. I considered that what we were hearing was outgoing. At that moment, a mortar landed close to where we were and I joined my friends on the floor. The mortaring continued. Then there was a lull. At that moment the troops ran to a shelter next door which also housed the dispensary and called me to follow. I did not give any lecture on the merits of that suggestion and was right behind them. Again, more mortars started falling on Cu Chi. We were safe now, protected by a heavily sandbagged metal shed. Then came a call over the line phone: one of the Bobcat barracks was hit and a number of casualties had been taken. Two of my medic friends raced to their jeep while mortars were still coming in. As the battalion chaplain, I considered it my duty to go with them to assist in any way I could. Being completely new at this business of mortar attacks I did not appreciate the danger involved.

As we drove to the area where help was needed I recall wondering when our return fire was going to start. Everything was coming in at this time but nothing was going out in the direction of the enemy fire. What were our people doing?

When we arrived at the barracks, I saw many of our new troops milling about as if in a daze. A lieutenant directed us to the barracks where "they" were while he struggled to help a wounded man out of a water-filled ditch. In entering the barracks I recall noticing an eerie silence. There was a strong odor of powder and burned materials. The front end of the barracks was a shambles. A short-timer's party was going on, I was told. A short-timer's party is something all the troops look forward to having. It is a private celebration with close friends when you are about ready to return home. This group in the barracks included two men who were to leave the next day and three other men scheduled to leave in a week.

With a flashlight, we searched the debris and soon spotted first one body and then another. One victim was still alive. He had difficulty breathing. His eyes were pleading for help. He opened his mouth as if to speak, but it filled with blood and he died moments later. More debris was removed, and the others were found. One was seriously wounded but still alive. The other was found dead with his eyes staring upward, a look of surprise and anguished recognition on his face. As we tried to move his body to the jeep, my hands several times slipped over his warm, blood-covered skin. I recall how muscular this young man was—strong and healthy, a good life before him—and in a moment he was dead, no longer with us. I would have to be a year in Vietnam to fully appreciate the tragedy of such a moment: to go through the day-in and day-out routine of facing the possibility of instant death; of writing to your loved ones

and telling them everything was going to be all right; of endur-
ing the anguish of knowing there were those who loved you
back home and who were therefore dying a little every day in
the fear of receiving word of your injury or death; of sweating
out those last few weeks; and then only a few hours to go—a
few hours and finally free from that land and its hardships; free
from its scorching heat; free to sleep once again in a real bed
with clean sheets and a soft pillow; free to eat when you felt
like it and whatever you wanted; free to walk down a street and
not look for a booby trap; free to go to sleep, and sleep—really
sleep; free to once again be with those you love; to be able to
look at a park or wooded area and not have to wonder if Charlie
was there waiting for you to get a little closer; free once again
to live. It would take a year of existing in Vietnam under combat conditions to fully realize the tragedy that took place just a
few moments ago.

We brought the wounded and the dead out to the jeep. Mortars were still dropping on Cu Chi, but not in our sector. I still
did not hear any return fire from our side.

Our jeep was headed toward the Division Dispensary. The
medic who was driving the jeep kept up a steady stream of cursing directed at the enemy mortar fire. The jeep was moving at
a high rate of speed over a rough road. I was in the back trying
to keep myself and one of the casualties from bouncing out of
the jeep. I yelled in an angered frightened tone, "When the hell
are our people going to answer their fire?" Enemy mortars were
still coming in but nothing was going out.

We finally arrived at the 25th Med Dispensary where a lot of
activity was going on. Cu Chi was being hit hard and casualties
were increasing. A doctor came out to check our people. They
were pronounced dead. We had lost all of them.

As we left to return to the Bobcat area, I noticed that no more
mortars were falling on Cu Chi and that our guns were finally
going into action. Perhaps the six-months' respite caught our
troops dull and sluggish. Perhaps during the six months new

crews replaced the experienced ones and they simply had some learning to do before they could be effective. Soon these crews would have quite a bit of practice, especially after the first Tet Offensive.

As we drove back to our area not too much was said. We were tired and deeply disappointed. We had lost our people. I remarked again on the slowness of our guns to answer the enemy fire. As I reflect on it, no doubt the crews were inexperienced. From a military or tactical standpoint, one of the problems intrinsic to the required one-year tour in Vietnam was that it took about a year to get to know the enemy and how to fight him. Then, just when you could have been a serious problem to him, you went back home and were replaced by green troops who would go ahead and duplicate many of the earlier mistakes. Some battalions which were feared by the VC soon became "easy game" to the enemy when the inexperience ratio grew greater and greater. There are some things that one learns that simply cannot be passed on by words in a training camp. Only experience with the experienced can bring it about; and when the experienced left for home, the new men were candidates for Charlie's scorecard.

A number of medics were at the battalion dispensary, and some people with trivial injuries were receiving first aid treatment. I had a scratch on my arm and was asked if I wanted to be written up. Some time ago I had been told that a Purple Heart medal can be had if you receive any kind of injury while under hostile fire. It seems some people racing to a shelter in a mortar raid would bang their head or stub their toe and that would suffice to merit the Purple Heart. There was little equity between that and a fellow with a stomach wound received from direct contact with the enemy. It was difficult for me to understand how people could be so counterfeit as to demand a Purple Heart for a scratch when there were others who would receive such a medal for serious wounds requiring a painful stay in a hospital. I have known people of all grades in the Army from the lowest to a rather high rank who took advantage of such a cheap pretext. I would have been ashamed to wear such a ribbon on my chest. Men who must convalesce in a hospital because of the seriousness of their wounds have earned that sign of honor, but the conditions for meriting the Purple Heart are evidently so broad that technically a scratch suffices as well as a crippling wound. It is shameful that a medal of such honor can be so easily abused by pseudo-heroes. The next time someone brags about his Purple Heart, ask him how long he was hospitalized. If he's a good friend, you might ask him to show you his scar, but don't ask too many probing questions. It might prove embarrassing.

six

Several weeks had passed since the heavy mortar attack an Cu Chi. Things were back to normal. According to my schedule, the time had come for me to visit the 5th Mech. One of its companies happened to be in the Boi Loi Woods—a sector where the VC were especially strong. The history of the action of our troops in the Boi Loi was always one where our men suffered severe casualties. Talking to the "E2's" and "Speedy 4's," who make up the largest portion of the combat troops, I found that their experiences were bad. Many of their buddies had been killed or maimed for life in those woods. Whenever they had to go to the Boi Loi, they expected it to be costly. The terrain was thick with foliage and trees, giving Charlie many hiding places.

Once, when tracker dogs were still being used by the battalions, a skirmish with the enemy occurred and some of the enemy were apparently wounded. Tracker dogs were called for by the commander to help the troops locate the supposedly fleeing enemy, These dogs did their job well, following the trail of blood, but they were not trained to alert when near the enemy as were the scout dogs. Charlie had the wounded soldier dragged right to a well-concealed machine gun bunker in the woods. Shortly, there followed the tracker dogs and American troops. The tracker dogs, their handlers, and several others of the pursuing troops were cut down. They had been lured right to that machine gun bunker without ever seeing it. The soil of the Boi Loi had claimed more American blood. So there was the Boi Loi: beautiful one moment; a nightmare the next.

Since one of the Mech companies was there, I decided to set out for the Boi Loi. Before Tet, I usually traveled by Chinook, but this time the opportunity was afforded me to go by "Bubble," a small tri-seater helicopter which was used mainly for flying the battalion commander over the Area of Operations to see how well the troops were progressing on their mission and to direct the battle from the air once troops made contact with the enemy. The battalion commanders normally would be allotted so many flying hours before the copter would have to be turned over to some other battalion commander for his turn at aerial observation and direction. On occasions there would be enough flying time left for the battalion commander to loan out the helicopter to one of his company commanders who would go aloft to check out an area where some of his troops might be going that evening on ambush.

It so happened the "Bubble" was being sent by the battalion commander to a company CO whose troops seemed to have stumbled on something important in the Boi Loi. There was space available and I was able to obtain a ride there. This was going in style for me, since travel on a Chinook was not only noisy, but you had long hours to wait in the sun before getting aboard.

On my way out to the Boi Loi, I began to have misgivings about my good fortune. For what ensued had me suspecting the copter pilot had lost his mind. First, a "Bird Dog" plane—a rather slow, single engine, single wing, cabined craft—flew precariously near us. Such a plane customarily would be employed to mark the spot where the enemy positions were described to the pilot by the American troops on the ground. Then the swift fighter-bombers, with whom the Bird Dog teamed, would jet in, bombing and strafing that smoked-marked position.

After this Bird Dog plane approached us, a kind of dog fight took place between the wing and rotor crafts. It was quite an experience. I would have enjoyed it more if I had known that the pilot had not gone out of his mind but was only playing. Unfortunately, I did not have the ear phones on and so did not know that the fellow in the Bird Dog was a buddy and this was some sort of game they would often play when they had the opportunity. The pilot mentioned this to the other occupant of the Bubble who went along with the little game, but as I was not in on it all I could think was that an air-to-air collision was only moments away. I thought to myself, "What a way to go. Being in Vietnam and getting zapped in the air. And by my own people, at that!" I must admit the helicopter pilot did surprisingly well, maneuvering his craft so as to often get on the tail of the plane. After what seemed like an hour the two decided that was it for the day and "Snoopy" continued on to Bravo Company in the Boi Loi, while the "Red Baron" disappeared in the direction of the Black Virgin Mountain.

Landing at Bravo Company's field position in the Boi Loi, I thanked the pilot for the ride and no longer felt so unkindly towards the Chinooks.

No sooner did I arrive than an invitation was extended me to go with a platoon of troops to an area not too far away where the rest of Bravo Company had located what appeared to be an enemy base camp. This would be quite a discovery. So off we went with the troops. I observed how rugged and thick the woods were. Any kind of fighting here could be costly.

As we moved forward in single file I asked one of the troops how it came about that this enemy location was found. He answered that some of the company were simply moving along on a routine search and destroy mission and would have passed right by the enemy, except that they fired on them thus disclosing their presence. Soon the enemy broke contact and in the subsequent pursuit the troops came upon what appears to be the base camp of this elusive enemy.

While we were making our way through the woods there was a group of GI's on our flanks who were not at all enjoying the scenery. It was their job to protect the flanks of the main column and so they were off the trail and had to make their own paths through the dense undergrowth. The going was slow. It was now late in the morning and the heat of the day was beginning to increase. Trying to hack their way through with machetes was an ordeal. This procedure is necessary, however, if you are to protect your main column from a possible wipeout by an enemy ambush. In most of the ambushes that the Americans were caught in, a careful study would show carelessness on someone's part about taking such proper security measures as this was responsible for the disastrous results that followed.

After about three-quarters of an hour, we came upon some of our troops who gave us further directions on the location of the base camp. I recall seeing a massive bomb crater made by a B-52. It measured about thirty feet in diameter and twenty feet deep. There were others craters around also but I soon saw that none of the bombs fell within the base camp.

When we reached the enemy base camp, I was astonished at how neat and clean everything was. The enemy was not there, but some warm rice was found indicating a caretaker group of the enemy had been there and left in a hurry. The company was instructed to search the base camp. Troops were moving about here and there. I decided to join in with the search and so wandered about the area to see what I could find.

The base camp of the enemy was well engineered. On the perimeter he had ribbons of trenches with holes dug into the walls. The function of these holes was to give him cover if grenades or shells should begin landing in his trenches in a fire fight. Once the shelling stopped, he could come out and fire away at the approaching troops who might think he had been clobbered only to find out too late that he was very much alive. Then, if you did get by these serpentine trenches, there were his bunkers to contend with, real masterpieces. First of all, these bunkers were extremely low to the ground with little slits from which they could fire. The solid bunker roof was made up of limbs and cement clay. The arrangement of the bunkers was such that each bunker could cover every other bunker. I could imagine some enterprising GI crawling up on one of those bunkers and never realizing until too late that another bunker some meters away he never noticed had a clear shot at him. The concealment was perfect. It was no wonder that troops could walk right over such bunkers and not even realize it. The thought occurred to me what an ugly time it would have been if the enemy had been here in force and decided to put up a fight. How many of our GI's would have been cut down? Today our boys had been fortunate in the Boi Loi Woods.

The insides of the enemy bunkers were also remarkable. Everyone I entered was clean. Many of them had a crude bench made of soft sapling boughs. One bunker I entered had a lower level into which you could take refuge from the concussion of shells if the bombardment came upon your area. I suspect that it was this kind of arrangement that the enemy used when so often our troops would go against a bunkered enemy after a fierce shelling, only to find the enemy firing away again just as heavily as before the shelling. Once the shells started dropping, the enemy knew that our troops would not be moving forward until the shelling stopped. So, they would simply go to the lower level of their bunkers and let the artillery fire away. Once the shelling ended they knew the GI's would be approaching and so they would crawl to the upper level of the bunker and be ready to cut them down when they came within range. A number of American officers were unhappy with this "hold routine" of the troops until the shelling ceased. I was told the usual tactical method was to have the troops move up behind the artillery barrage and so be right on top of the enemy by the time the shelling stopped. The account I heard was that this tactic was not permitted because of the possibility of American casualties. The word was out that Washington wanted casualties held down to the minimum to mollify the growing resentment of groups back in the States against the war. In a fight of this nature, however, you can't hold back and expect to come out without a bruise. As a result of this overcautious approach, the troops found themselves actually in a worse situation since the artillery support would not be fully effective without their progressive follow up.

All during my year in Vietnam, I recall the same approach being used when contact was made with a bunkered enemy, with the same ineffectual results. The routine generally went like this: Fire support was requested upon contact being made with the enemy. First came the helicopter gunships who fired off their small rockets and sprayed the enemy occupied area with machine gun fire. While such an attack was lethal to an enemy caught out in the open, it was inconsequential against a well-bunkered enemy. Then came an air strike followed by the artillery barrage. With phase one of the attack plan completed, we are now ready for phase two: the troop assault. Once our troops moved into the enemy zone, they would be fired upon and some of our men would be instantly killed and others wounded. Surprised at the enemy's fire power, our troops would soon find themselves being forced back. More fire support was then requested by our forces. The enemy would again retreat to the lower level of the bunkers and wait for the shelling to stop. After this he would come up and go through a replay of the former show with the ironically expendable American troops taking it on the chin again and again. Soon we only wanted to get our dead out of the enemy zone. So more of the same routine: air strikes and copter attacks followed by artillery and then forward with the troops. Experienced officers told me that fewer lives would have been lost if they had been permitted to move the troops up behind the shelling, but well meaning people back in the States were putting political pressure on the powers that be and so the Army had no choice but to obey. Being now inside one of those bunkers, I could better appreciate the enemy's advantage. Of course it would have been suicide to retreat to the lower level of the bunker if our troops were right behind the shelling where they could immediately overrun his fortifications. As it was our troops seldom had such an opportunity and such skirmishes usually ended with the Americans taking casualties, expending a great deal of futile fire power and having next to nothing to show for it. At night, the enemy would steal away. The next morning the Americans would return and cautiously retrieve their dead, finding that the enemy had gone.

I found myself inspecting quite a number of bunkers. As I think of it, we were fortunate that the enemy did not have time to set up any booby traps there. While I was somewhat cautious in entering those bunkers, nonetheless my inexperience exposed me to serious mishap. While our troops are given instructions on mines and booby traps, as a chaplain, I never received any such introduction. What I had heard from talking with the troops, I tried to put into practice. When, for instance, I saw a gleaming shovel head directly within the entrance of a bunker, I made no attempt to go and pick it up. First I found a long enough branch with which to move the shovel head, while giving myself cover alongside the entrance. If a hand grenade were set to go off under that shovel when once moved, there would be no danger of injury. As nothing happened, I cautiously entered the bunker, looking for any string or wire which might also be used to trip off an explosive. Once within the bunker, I waited for my eyes to become accustomed to the dim light. The darker areas of the place I checked out with a pen flashlight. A metal object was found hidden within the sapling bench. It turned out to be a native ax head. Further investigation came up with some handwritten sheets of paper slightly charred along the edges, some apparently inconsequential pieces of cardboard which perhaps was makeshift scratch paper and a plastic case with a couple of photographs of men and some cards—all of which I turned over to intelligence.

Later I found myself teamed up with several GI's and a lieutenant. We came upon the enemy kitchen area with its tunnel system to dissipate the smoke when they cooked. We also found their latrine area which would have pleased the most demanding of sanitation inspectors. While continuing the search one of our enlisted men discovered some empty cans on which was printed a United States emblem. It turned out these were cans of oil for cooking and were supplied by the Americans to their allies. In Cu Chi there was a section of the base camp called "Helping Hand," which functioned as a warehouse area for any food stuffs which were to go to the Vietnamese people. As often happened, such food would soon end up in the hands of the VC who would pay their night visits to the villages and acquire the food they needed either through political allegiance to the communist cause or by the threat of their weapons. It was ironic to think we were helping to feed the enemy. I was to find out there were many things we were doing, unconsciously or through carelessness, to help the enemy.

The GI's with me finally called a halt to the search to have a bite to eat. The VC had fashioned a table and benches out of tree limbs and we gratefully utilized their facilities. For a moment I thought I was back in the States at a picnic. Many years earlier I had been a Boy Scout and used to go camping. Little did I think then I would ever be in an Oriental country camping, much less feasting on C Rations! I was surprised how pleasant the weather was in these woods. The trees parried the unrelenting thrusts of the sun and I found myself unusually comfortable. A cool breeze was working its way through the woods. Even the air had a refreshing smell to it. The young lieutenant spoke about having recently finished college and of his hopes to return to his wife and begin making a life for himself. The two enlisted men were not too talkative. The lieutenant was a recent addition to the company and not knowing much about him they were naturally cautious.

Returning again to the search we came upon a well. We were told the commanding officer was there earlier and threw a smoke grenade into the well but that nothing further was done. Since the enemy had been known to store weapons within sealed containers in rivers and streams the lieutenant decided to investigate the well. A long sapling was used to prod the well bottom. The GI's noticed that there was the sensation of some hard object below the water's surface. The lieutenant told one of the GI's to go down into the well and check it out. As he began to take off some of his combat gear, I suggested to the lieutenant that I go down since I was traveling light. The lieutenant was surprised, but agreed. I grabbed onto the makeshift pole and started down. As I descended I noticed foot holes along the side of the well wall. I yelled this up to the group. They were enthused. Perhaps we would come upon something. I finally reached the water and went in. I had forgotten to take out of my pockets an inexpensive camera and my wallet. Fortunately, they were wrapped up in a plastic bag and so kept dry. Such use of a plastic covering was popular with the ground troops, and now I knew why. There was a chill to the water. My friends above called down and asked how I was. With a chatter, my voice replied, "OK."

Reaching the bottom of the well, my boots sank about six inches in the mucky bottom. To check the objects I was feeling with my boots, it was necessary to go under. My whole body shivered from the cold water. All I came up with were more empty oil cans, nothing else. The lieutenant called me to come up. Grabbing on our makeshift pole, I began the journey upward. I thought I was in good shape but found myself exhausted half way up. Twice my feet slipped off the slimy walls and I began to wonder if I could make it to the top. Those above were encouraging me to reach their outstretched hands. For a moment I felt I was going to lose my grip and fall back into the well. The thought of inconveniencing my friends, however, meant more to me than my weariness. I said a hasty prayer and gave a strong effort to reach their saving hands. They grabbed hold of me just as my strength left me altogether. At this point I was helpless. If their hands would have slipped, I would have dropped right back into that well. Their hands were sure, however, and they pulled me up.

Then they all looked at me strangely for a moment, and then began to laugh. I was covered totally in purple. The smoke bomb that had been thrown in the well earlier had been a purple marker. My hands, arms, face and clothes were purple. I then realized why it was I became so weak in trying to climb out of the well. My lungs must have had a large degree of that purple smoke in it and so there was less oxygen. Months later we would learn several Americans lost their lives going down a well. A GI first went down to wash and collapsed. A second and third GI went down to help him and also collapsed. All three were dead when rescue operations began in earnest. An investigation proved negative. Perhaps there were earth gasses down there. Whatever it was, three men died. As I look back on my experience I now realize how fortunate I was. But then, when I consider that earlier I was alone and unarmed going through enemy bunkers, what would I have done if a VC was in one of them? It didn't happen and I was grateful.

An hour or so had passed when our group had come upon some other GI's at an entrance to one of the VC tunnels. This entrance was unusually narrow and they were looking for someone small enough to enter since their sizes qualified them to be on a pro football team. I was the smallest and they asked if I would care to go in and see what could be found. I told them I was willing to try. Inside the tunnel there was a small lower entry way. It was hot and I felt as if I were in a tomb. Finding some vials, I passed them out to the troops. I never did know if they were of any importance. Moving about in such cramped quarters was fatiguing and I was happy to crawl out.

The lieutenant reported this tunnel and it was marked to be blown up along with the rest of the tunnels and bunkers. An engineer group was flown in by chopper and began to set the dynamite charges. We were to move out on the double. As I left that VC base camp, it was hard to believe that almost seven hours had gone by. It seemed like a few minutes. When the other troops of Bravo Company saw me, they were dumbfounded. For the hues of yellow, brown, black and white were common in Vietnam, but whoever expected to see a person who was purple? The troops enjoyed it and I certainly felt like I belonged to them now. No longer did I wear an immaculate set of fatigues. I was now as soiled looking as the rest of them. For a few hours I shared in something that was their everyday lot. It may not have been much, but their faces told me they approved. I was better able to appreciate their condition, and no longer would be among that long list of people who claimed to be concerned about them and their welfare, but who never sought to take the steps to understand their condition. I am sure that if many of those in power had made such an effort they would never have done what they did to our troops in the name of political expediency.

When we arrived back at Bravo Company's field position, I ate with the troops and then held a service. This was the highlight of my day: being able to worship God and to pray for my troops, all of them, that they would have the strength to bear the continued tension that is a combat soldier's life.

It was now late evening. I would sleep deeply that night and yet I felt somewhat guilty as I rested on the ground. For me to be able to sleep someone would have to be awake during the night.

25th infantry division general headquarters, Cu Chi, Vietnam. We are told the enemy used the two American flagpoles as sighting objects firing rockets at this building.

A chaplain stands before this 45th surgical field hospital known as a MUST (mobile unit surgical transportable), which also had its own chapel facilities. Such units stabilized the seriously wounded before they were helicoptered to advanced hospitalization facilities away from the firefight zones.

Chaplain's assistant Wally Nelson stands before the entrance to the bunker he helped the battalion chaplain of the 5th Mech construct after the chaplain's hooch (living quarters) was destroyed when an enemy rocket hit an adjacent ammo dump, flattening the entire battalion area.

Chaplain Falabella in full field gear has arrived at the helicopter supply field, "row bravo," after serving his troops in the field for the past five days.

An example of the wet living conditions in the field during the monsoon months in 3rd Corps area in Vietnam. The ground, inundated for a thousand years by water buffalo dung, gives off an offensive stench that I have never forgotten.

Weary infantry boarding trucks after a battle in the Hoc Mon area, during the first Tet Offensive.

Chaplain Falabella (left), Captain Theologus, Commander Charlie Company (center), and Sergeant Long, Vietnamese interpreter, with nuns who care for orphaned children at the convent in the Cholon district of Saigon. After a lull from the first Tet Offensive, much-needed food was brought to the orphaned children.

seven

Having held the regular Sunday services at Cu Chi, I was on my way to the 5th Mech field position. Being with the Mech was always a treat, since it meant that I had up to three days to spend with them in the field before having to leave to go after the Wolfhounds. Getting out to the Hounds necessitated much preparation with my gear, as well as the expenditure of precious time in simply trying to reach them. Once there, much physical work was required to dig a foxhole and set up sleeping facilities. Normally all this labor, once done, would be good for the stay of the battalion in that place, but since I had to move out the next morning I would find myself repeating the entire routine in the new battalion area, again just for one night. The procedure with the Hounds was a grueling one.

When I went to the 5th Mech, however, I could travel much lighter, needing only the poncho liner and the service kit and could enjoy the field facilities of the battalion doctor and his senior medic team. This meant I had a place to sleep, namely, in the "Big Angel" track which was the battalion medical vehicle. It was at this vehicle location that medical aid was dispensed to the troops. If a sickness required convalescence in a hospital, the doctor would have the patient sent to Cu Chi. In field emergency cases, however, away from the battalion camp, the doctor would be bypassed by the "Dust Off" (medic helicopter ships) which would fly the wounded soldier immediately to established hospital facilities, such as those at Cu Chi. It was for this reason that some of the battalion doctors I spoke with were against the concept of battalion field doctors. They were of the opinion that such a concept had validity when the helicopter did not exist and there was only the field hospital as the condition *sine qua non* if the wounded was to have any chance at all for survival. But with the advent of the helicopter a wounded soldier could often be picked up within minutes and brought to a completely equipped hospital. If more sophisticated treatment was necessary, the wounded man could be flown in hours to Japan or the United States.

The present system of medical treatment was remarkable and the troops derived much confidence from it. If you had the misfortune to get hit but not killed, you had a ninety-eight percent chance of surviving. Besides the swift transportation and advanced medical facilities, the troops also had their medics (whom they called "doc") whose courage and sacrifices could fill many tomes. Out in combat the troops knew their medics were there. If you were hit you'd yell "medic" or "doc" and you could be sure he would be by your side or die trying. His getting there quickly could well mean your life for he was trained to stop the bleeding, without which subsequent aid is of little use. It was the medic's job to try and keep you alive long enough to reach the professional hands of the doctors and the nurses. The troops I knew all praised their medics highly.

With the medics near you in battle, with the helicopter "Dust Off" ships on alert to serve as an air ambulance, and with an outstanding medical structure set up all the way to the States, the GI knew he had a lot going for him. It was because of such a system that some of the battalion field doctors I spoke with felt their talents were wasted in the field. Most of the time they were dispensing pills which the medics could be doing just as well while back at the hospitals there could be emergency rush periods when more doctors might mean more lives saved. Those extra doctors, they contended, were out in the field perhaps reading a paperback to stave off the boredom of having next to nothing to do.

On the other hand I heard that one advantage of having the doctor in the field with the battalion was that as an experienced medical authority he could ascertain whether a soldier there had a serious enough reason for leaving the field and returning to Cu Chi for medical help or not. In short, the battalion doctor out in the field could intercept any soldier attempting to "goldbrick" his way out of field duties by returning to the Cu Chi Dispensary for a time-consuming check-up. If a rash of such "goldbricking" took place, the strength of the individual companies would be seriously impaired. By having a doctor in the field, it was felt this could be prevented. It is not as easy to criticize the diagnosis of a doctor as it would be that of a medic when it came to simply "not feeling well." So I suspect that this field roster situation had something to do with keeping those doctors out there, despite the revolutionary changes brought about by the helicopter ambulance. Perhaps by now that controversial arrangement has been changed.

The 5th Mech was presently pacifying the Thai My area which was about a ten minute copter ride from Cu Chi. Before the Mech came into Thai My, the area was heavily infiltrated with VC. The persistent presence of the Mech helped in great measure to clear that area, although not completely.

One day the battalion commander decided to have a "Med Cap" in Thai My village. It seemed the village was sufficiently free of VC presence to do this. A Med Cap was an operation to try and give medical help to the village people. Often of course VC and their families would receive the benefits of such a medical activity, since how could any American really know who was VC and who wasn't?

The doctor and senior medics of the Big Angel track invited me, as their guest, to accompany them to the village. I readily accepted. The procedure of entering a village for the first time was interesting. Leaving the doctor and his medics at the village school to prepare for the Med Cap, the battalion civil-affairs officer and his interpreter walked down the main street of the village. Using a bull horn they called out to the villagers to come out of their homes. No one was going to hurt them and the Americans had a doctor who would give free medical treatment to them and their children. Now as the Thai My area still had some VC about, a platoon of soldiers lined up on both sides of the street and accompanied us. They did not, however, go storming into the village huts on both sides of the street to check for a possible ambush. This made the situation somewhat chancy. When we reached the end of the village, we returned to the school where our medical people were now ready. In a short time villagers began to come timidly forward to bring their sick to the doctor and the medics. I recall an extremely old man being carried by two younger people to the doctor who diagnosed he was dying and gave some medicine to lessen his pain.

Soon I left the school area and started on walking down what would be side streets and looking at the different village huts. I smiled at the occupants who were cautiously peering from within and found myself wanting to speak with them, be with them, and come to understand them. Perhaps they sensed this. Some came out and invited me into their little dwellings. Inside I found they had the barest necessities: plain simple furniture of heavy coarse wood, with oil lamps to provide light in the evenings. The floor consisted of the bare ground with straw mats as bedding. I tried to communicate with the people with the few words of Vietnamese I knew. A villager came forward and began speaking broken English. He became my interpreter and I was then able to speak with the people. It was a warm experience. As I was leaving to go to another dwelling where I was invited, some of our troops came up to me with anxious faces and said they were sent to find me and bring me back to the main area. As I went back with them some of the villagers I was talking with came along also, among them my newly-found interpreter.

Upon my return to the school area I decided to ask the villagers about a church building that was set back about fifty meters from the main street. With the help of my interpreter, I found out that it was a Catholic church but that the priest had fled from the VC. As a result there had been no services conducted in the church for many months. I noticed ugly bullet holes in the walls and doors of the church. I then pointed to the cross on my shirt collar and said "Cha," which meant "Father." When the children and adults who were standing around me heard this and finally understood through the interpreter that I was a priest, they became enthused and began talking at the same time. The children were jumping up and down. I asked my recently acquired friend what was happening and he replied that the people were rejoicing because a priest had come to their village and that now they could again worship their God in church. "They wish you to say Mass for them," the interpreter said. I opened the large church door and went in. The growing crowd followed me. I noticed some small holes in the roof but outside of that the church was in good condition. There were crude benches for pews and a large bell in the tower. When I left the church I told the people through the interpreter that I would ask permission from the American commander to hold a religious service for anyone in the village who might wish to attend. As soon as I had an answer I would inform them of it.

Returning to our battalion base camp at the end of the Med Cap, which turned out well for a first attempt, I reported the events to the commanding officer. He was in favor of holding the religious service, but no definite date could be given for obvious security reasons. I was to report to the people that some time in the future such a service would be held.

The villagers did not have too long to wait. The following week, when I returned to the 5th Mech at Thai My, the commanding officer informed me that he would send a platoon of soldiers to act as security for a special civil-affairs operation that would take place that afternoon in the village. It would be my job to conduct the religious services there, as requested.

No sooner did we enter the village than a small crowd of Vietnamese gathered around. Some folded their hands as though in prayer and then pointed to the service kit I was carrying on my shoulder. I nodded. Their eyes grew wide and bright. Two ran off to the church, and soon its bells were ringing wildly.

I noticed many of our troops smiling. They had been told the nature of this operation. They were to give security for anyone who might be attending a service in the village church. This was a civil-affairs action to show the good will of the Americans. Our country had a history of freedom of worship. Those Vietnamese who so wished were going to have the opportunity to worship as they pleased, at least for today.

The troops took their defensive positions around the church which had been searched earlier for booby traps. As I entered the church and started vesting, a good-sized crowd was developing. As it turned out not only were Catholics there but also Buddhists. I would find that they were as pleased as the Catholics that a religious service was taking place. After all, the people in this village were friends. The Buddhists were happy in knowing that their fellow villagers were receiving some measure of happiness from this religious service. As usual, there is no problem with genuine people in matters of religious differences. The problem is elsewhere with a handful of self-appointed judges on both sides who contradict, by their lack of charitable understanding, everything they supposedly represent.

The service was about to begin and I had a surprise for those within the church. Some time before I came over as a chaplain with the infantry, I had said several Masses for the Vietnamese in the little village of Trang Bang. The people were polite at the service, but here was an American in Vietnam saying a Mass in Latin! How much better it would be if an American were to say the Mass in Vietnamese. This would certainly show goodwill on our part, and perhaps enable the people to be more natural in their prayer. For this reason, while I was with Support Command, I studied how to read a Mass in Vietnamese through the help of a native priest who taped the prayers for me. I had yet to actually conduct such a service in Vietnamese, however, because I feared causing confusion rather than edification. But now I decided to hazard the service in Vietnamese.

Using a small Vietnamese Mass pamphlet, I sang aloud the initial prayers of the service. I expected the people to roar with laughter at my feeble attempt to read their language but instead, after a pause of evident surprise, they all chimed right in with the response. From that moment on the Mass was indeed their own. The people had a drum and some stringed instrument which they used with their singing. I would intone the beginning of a prayer, and they would then follow right along with it, singing beautifully in their quaint high tones.

When the service was over the people were incredibly happy. The Americans had come and they were enabled to worship their God, after being deprived of this for so long. As I passed through them, there were tears of gratitude in their eyes. I never experienced people so joyful and excited. Our troops, guarding outside, thankfully had no incidents to mar the happiness of the occasion. It seemed that in the faces of our troops there was a sense of accomplishment that day. Seldom does a soldier see what good may come from his presence. That day they saw it and were rightfully proud. They brought joy to a people in need and could see it in the people's faces, a consolation seldom experienced by a combat soldier in Vietnam.

eight

Christmas

Christmas away from home is usually not a happy occasion. When you are in a foreign land where you may be killed the next moment, such a holiday season accentuates your trying situation. For the combat troops in the field Christmas day was a painful experience. A "truce" has been declared which means you will not be fighting the enemy unless he attacks you. Your every day experience is to go after him and as a result you become accustomed to the pressure and the strain. But now, during the truce, you must wait and see. When you have nothing but one disappointment after another in the field, you are not too anxious to have yourself exposed to the added one of having your hopes for a day's respite from the fighting shattered by the enemy killing one of your closest friends.

The troops I spoke with considered the "truce" a time Charlie could safely move about and prepare lethal harassment against them with impunity. As usual there seemed to be no one to champion the viewpoint of the troops. People who were not involved with the actual fighting were dictating what was best for the troops. The desire to be shown humane overrode the realistic exigencies of the situation and was a further example of a too prevalent appraisal of war in romantic and chivalrous terms.

Christmas in the field was grim. I recall the troops using a bush in their vicinity as a Christmas tree. While some approached the trimming of the tree in the customary manner by placing on the branches the cards and candy canes sent from home, other troops trimmed the tree with objects depicting the circumstances of their immediate environment, including belts of machine gun ammo, grenades, smoke bomb canisters, empty cans of soda pop and a lieutenant's bars at the top of the bush. At the base was a claymore mine.

The boys tried to smile when I came around but I could see it was difficult for them. One consolation was a terrific dinner with turkey, cranberry sauce, mashed potatoes, peas, salad, cocktail nuts and an ice cream sundae. This was certainly a remarkable gustatory distraction which contrasted sharply with their immediate surroundings. As I saw the troops feasting during this "truce" period, pity for them flooded my heart. "Here is the best your country can do for you. Eat up, gentlemen!" And indeed they did. The condemned ate a hearty meal.

My Introduction to the 122

It was now late January and something was afoot. Our troops were moving farther and farther from Saigon. Supposedly the enemy was being driven out of Vietnam. As one officer put it, we were now pacifying the jungles. Meanwhile the enemy was quietly preparing his first Tet Offensive which came close to taking Saigon itself.

An indication of a change was in the kind of fire power the enemy was beginning to employ in their attacks on main base camps, using the 122 rocket. My first experience with this rocket I will never forget.

During January Cu Chi was again receiving night mortar attacks. Whenever the alert sounded, I simply rolled to the floor of my quarters. I never bothered to go to the shelter across the road since I felt that the chance of getting hit while on my way to the shelter was about the same as being hit in my quarters. On this night some enemy mortars fell on Cu Chi and I rolled on to the floor until it seemed to stop. At the all clear I went back to bed. A few minutes passed and then it happened. A shrill, pressurized hissing sound was heard. Whatever it was it seemed to be moving at tremendous speed. Instinctively I sensed danger and sprang out of my bed for the floor. Before I reached it the 122 rocket struck about sixty-five meters from my quarters. The explosion was sharp and deafening. This was an ordnance sound I had never heard before and it was terrifying. Three more times that dread, shrill wild hissing went over my quarters and hit in our area. By this time I had crawled under my metal desk with my arms shielding my head. Never had I felt as helpless as at that moment. I felt as though I were disintegrating. It was an experience unknown to me. Nor would I ever become really used to that 122 rocket, no matter how many more times I went through a repetition of such attacks. Again the rockets thundered. These seemed to be coming right into my quarters. I found myself saying over and over, "My God, my God, what is it?" Then quiet suddenly settled over us. I decided to crawl to the bunker across the road. Mortars were one thing but these rockets were something else.

When I arrived at the shelter I found some other officers of the area there. Someone said, "How are you doing, Chaplain? Join the group." Then the battalion doctor spoke up in an excited tone. "Did you know that one of those rockets landed right in the barracks where I was sleeping? It knocked me right the hell out of bed but I was untouched. I still have the ringing in my ears." I peered at him incredulously and wondered how he possibly survived. A lieutenant decided to inspect the damaged barracks. The doctor and I went with him. At the barracks we saw that the rocket crashed into the forward part of the building. Fortunately for the doctor a large bookcase separated his cubicle from where the explosion occurred. The concussive force of the rocket made a complete shambles of the other quarters but was evidently dissipated by the large bookcase-divider. The bed in which the doctor slept collapsed, throwing him to the floor. We noticed that his mattress was in flames. Hot shrapnel had hit it but somehow missed the doctor.

Later, we would discover more about that rocket from subsequent attacks. For one thing, its concussive force was more severe than first suspected. A sergeant, for instance, was sleeping in the barracks of another battalion when a rocket attack occurred. One landed near him. After the attack his body was found but there were no shrapnel marks nor visible wounds. Yet he was dead. In his case there was nothing to dissipate the shock waves. It turned out his lungs had been collapsed by the explosive concussion. Bunkers that could protect from mortars were inadequate against these 122 rockets and would have to be quite substantially reinforced to provide effective cover. While the rocket lacked pinpoint accuracy, it did have a sizable destructive as well as demoralizing value. The use of such rockets against cities like Saigon therefore could only be for the purpose of indiscriminate destruction. The 122 rocket was a potent weapon in the arsenal of the VC and North Vietnamese and added to their ability to place the South Vietnamese government and the American troops in an awkward position. For the enemy could call the time and place for the destructive assaults, all of which took place in South Vietnam. Every time the South Vietnamese government forces and the American troops fought back, they would find themselves in the embarrassing position of furthering the destruction of the land they were pledged to defend. It was a terrible dilemma,

The Tet Offensive Begins

The attacks of the enemy were now increasing. I was with the 1st of the 27th Wolfhounds who were summoned to investigate some suspicious movements near Saigon. The rest of the battalions were a good distance away. Then it happened. The Hounds were ordered to go immediately to an area around Hoc Mon where the enemy had shown up in great force and were taking over a village. The enemy would soon be taking over many villages all over South Vietnam, for it was the beginning of their Tet Offensive. I was told to return to Cu Chi. When I arrived there by Chinook my assistant informed me that heavy contact with the enemy was being made everywhere and that the roads to Cu Chi were under their control. It would take severe fighting before the roads were once again opened up for daylight travel. Information came in of the enemy attacking on the wire at Tan Son Nhut; of the enemy being in parts of Saigon and attacking the American Embassy. Up and down South Vietnam, reports came in of enemy activity. This was a full scale all out offensive by the North Vietnamese and the VC. General Westmoreland, speaking to the troops over the Armed Forces Radio, put it succinctly: "The enemy were going for broke."

In the IIIrd Corps Area, most of the mechanized troops were far to the west, and had to be rushed down to Hoc Mon and Saigon. A vital goal of the enemy offensive in this area was to blow up the Hoc Mon bridge to slow down our mechanized forces in getting to Saigon. The failure of the enemy to destroy the bridge enabled a mechanized unit, the 3/4 Cav, to break up the assault at the edge of the Tan Son Nhut airbase, which otherwise certainly would have fallen. It would take a couple of months of intense fighting before the situation would again be under control.

Cu Chi was still under considerable harassment by the enemy. The 4th of the 23rd mechanized infantry was sent out to lessen their influence on the neighboring area. The base camp for the mechanized unit was within sight of Cu Chi. I recall an early morning attack against their perimeter. I had visited with this group the evening before and expected to leave for Cu Chi that day. Suddenly, a mortar and ground assault was launched against the camp. Within minutes, a message was received from one of the counter-mortar areas that a GI was wounded. The battalion doctor immediately took a litter and left the medic track to go to the GI. Since it takes two to carry a litter, I followed after him. It was edifying to see this doctor risking his entire medical future by exposing himself to mortar fire in order to help a wounded GI. The distance to be covered was substantial, but we reached it safely. The doctor decided to carry the wounded man back to the medical track once the attack subsided. There the wound was treated and a helicopter medic ship was requested to ferry the wounded soldier to one of our hospitals near Saigon.

Some of our troops were sent out in pursuit of the retreating enemy. Over the radio we could hear the young lieutenant calling back his progress and the commanding officer trying to reduce his overanxiousness in pursuit. Some time later I was to hear that this young officer was killed in a similar situation. Soon a track was sent outside the wire to police up the enemy dead who were suited in coarse blue uniforms and wearing Ho Chi Minh sandals. Their bodies were stacked up on top of one another inside one of the larger tracks. It was a gruesome sight, as are the vestiges of any combat.

With the pressure and feelings of the early morning attack still fresh in my mind, I was anxiously looking towards the Cu Chi base camp, which I heard on the receiver was undergoing a rocket attack. Suddenly a tremendous cloud of black smoke appeared in that direction. The enemy had hit an ammo dump. Further information described the area hit as just across from the 5th Mech battalion area. I knew that ammo dump well, since I lived directly across the street from it. First reports were that the battalion area was demolished. Fortunately the majority of the battalion were out in the field, but the loss in matériel was extensive.

Later in the morning a Chinook returned me to Cu Chi where my assistant filled me in on just what had happened. The first rocket attacks came late in the evening. One of the rockets landed a few feet from where I would have been sleeping had I been in Cu Chi that night. My quarters were demolished and a medic rushed there thinking I was under the rubble. Fortunately I wasn't. I was out with the 4th of the 23rd because of a request from that battalion's chaplain that those troops of his that were Catholic have the opportunity of religious services. Then that morning, while I was still away from Cu Chi, another rocket attack hit the ammo dump with consequent destruction of almost all of the 5th Mech area. When I arrived at the Bobcat area, I was astounded by the devastation. My former quarters were totally demolished as was the dispensary next door, I was advised to stay away from my quarters since live explosives could be under the debris. The entire area would first have to be cleared by the explosives and demolition teams before anyone could safely live in that section of the camp. After I was given the go-ahead to return, I came upon an explosive shell which had been overlooked while I was clearing away the wreckage.

It was evident my quarters would have to be entirely rebuilt. Since this was true for the battalion area I knew my place would be last on the list. I decided I had better take care of myself. It's a good thing I did since it was not until June that the battalion was able to build new quarters for the battalion chaplain. This took several months and occurred only after every other building in the area was restored. By Tet I came to expect no favors from anyone and so was never disappointed.

I decided to build a foxhole-bunker. This would be far more substantial than what I could make for myself when out in the field. This project was done in the following way. First I dug a hole about three and a half feet deep and almost grave size in length. I would sleep next to this hole on the surface of the ground in a medic litter which was given me since it was ripped. Surrounding my foxhole and sleeping area were sandbags three deep in thickness. The ceiling of my sleeping quarters was about four feet high from ground level. The ceiling contained strips of metal runway, called SP, topped off by sandbags. Inside a mosquito net was fastened which completely enclosed the litter. This net gave me added security not only from mosquitoes but from the large rats that ran around at night. If a mortar attack occurred I'd remain right where I was. Even if the bunker were hit I felt quite secure. If rockets came in, my bunker could not sustain a direct hit but you could always roll into the foxhole along side the litter as a last resort.

For me this kind of living was a luxury since I could never have as fine a foxhole as this in the field. I really felt relaxed there and would write my weekly letter home by candlelight. From that time in early February until the middle of June when I was transferred to the artillery, I never knew what it was to again sleep in any kind of bed. I always slept fully clothed and with my boots on, just as in the field. The advantage of getting in on weekends was that I could at least get washed. Whenever I would go out to the field I'd place some boards at the entrance of my bunker so as to keep the many dogs that roamed about Cu Chi from taking up squatter's rights in my living quarters.

I still needed some shelter for my clothes and supplies. With the help of my assistant I built a typical looking shack near my sleeping quarters from pieces of wood scrounged up from the earlier explosion. The battalion authorities were not too keen on my shack. It looked ludicrous, especially in contrast to both the flattened area all around and the new buildings now going up here and there, but I let all their hints as to "that eyesore" go right over me. Not receiving consideration from them was understandable since there were more pressing priorities, but to take away my little shack was something else. Nobody, but nobody, was going to touch my little shack. That poor shack—it was so pathetic looking. Perhaps even Charlie felt sorry for me because while mortars and rockets continued to come into the Bobcat area, not one ever came near my humble shack.

nine

A Decision Is Made

A question I had been pondering for some time was resolved at the time of Tet, namely, whether or not I should carry a weapon. The Army regulation simply stated that a chaplain would not be required to carry a weapon. The front office of the Chaplaincy said not to carry a weapon. For a while I did accept as unfitting a man "of the cloth" carrying a weapon. I even considered not carrying a weapon a sign of courage, but as the months passed my conversations with the troops caused me to question the validity of such a viewpoint. I realized that I had taken an opinion for granted and never analyzed it. GI's would come up to me and ask, "Chaplain, do you think God will forgive me?" When I inquired what they meant they would reply, "Do you think God will forgive me for killing the people we are fighting?" I would reply there was a difference between killing and murder. If someone attacked you, you had a right to defend yourself to the degree necessary. If in your act of defense death occurred, the act causing it would not be murder, which is the unjust taking of another's life and clearly a moral evil as well as a physical evil, but would be "killing" which, while not a moral evil, is clearly a physical evil and naturally abhorrent to human feelings and sensitivities. But the abhorrence of "killing" should not be confused with the question of its morality, which deals with reason and not primarily feelings.

For instance, if someone feels good while robbing people that does not make such an act just or right. So also, if someone "dislikes" the law or "feels" uncomfortable about it, that does not in itself make the law wrong or unjust. If "feelings" determined morality, then whatever was done by anyone on "feeling" would be "right," and this would lead to sheer chaos with its necessary threat to the peace, order and common good of society.

Invariably the next question would be, "But what of the commandment 'Thou shalt not kill'?" While interpretations of the Bible varied, it seemed reasonable to consider that the concept of "kill" in this Commandment had to do with "unjust" killing since not all incidents of killing in the Bible are condemned. It would seem there is a valid distinction between murder and killing. In a situation of combat, you are clearly defending yourself since wearing a military uniform and bearing a weapon make you liable to enemy fire. Whatever else you may think of war theoretically, the fact is you are here on the field of battle and not safely seated in a classroom discussing subtleties about taking another's life. Unless you defend yourself you will not only jeopardize your own life but also the lives of your comrades, since fire power can make the difference in who will live and who will die. You say you do not want to kill. Who "wants" to kill and is truly a sane man? But if you do not fire your weapon with the intention of being effective, you could be a factor in your buddies getting killed. In effect, you would be killing your own people.

When I finished, the GI's would look at me and say, "What you have said is interesting, chaplain, but I do not see you carrying a gun." The more I thought about that, the more it did seem to me a contradiction. Is there something morally wrong in carrying a weapon? Is it morally wrong for me to do what they are doing? If it is, then it must also be for them because I am no different from them. I am a man, a human being, just as they are. That I am a priest or preacher makes me by, that title alone, no more a man of God than any other man or woman on earth, for we are all the people of God. Do I believe it is wrong for these men to carry weapons and use them under these conditions here in Vietnam? I honestly did not. Then why should it be wrong, morally or otherwise, for me to carry a weapon? The environment I am in is no different from theirs. As a clergyman, I am bound to the same set of rules as any other man. Merely being a clergyman does not make me better than anyone else. My being better or worse will be to the extent I am true to the nature and capacities God had given me as a human being. The world is so obsessed with the hypocrisy of the double standard in so many facets of life that it seems to have imposed this phenomenon on the already unrealistically devised description of what a clergyman is supposed to be, something other than human.

As for the notion of "killing," there seems to be an assumed premise there that death is the worst of evils. Perhaps that is true if there is no God and if there is nothing after this life. But I believe there is a God, and His revelation made it clear that the worst of evils was not death, that is, not physical evil, but rather being in hell, moral evil and all it implies in the degradation of the human spirit. Sooner or later all men must die the physical death. The important thing is how did you live your physical life? How did you come to understand and appreciate the mystery of yourself as being in the image of God? How honestly did you accept the mystery of yourself in its relationship to God, as demonstrated by your willingness to sacrifice everything, even your physical life, for your belief in the deeper destiny of man; a destiny which transcends the grave and which is tested by your "living" certain principles in this life which are considered of such value that physical death itself is preferred to capitulation?

What I am to become in the future is being worked out now in the present. In this world there are many possibilities opened to man—many political ideologies, many ways to live and to love. There will necessarily be some apparently irreconcilable viewpoints that might explode into violent confrontation. Each man must be true to himself in his search for what is "real." And so I am not surprised that the VC and North Vietnamese fight with the determination they do. They believe in what they are fighting for. But what of me? Do I know, much less believe, in what I represent? They are willing to die for what they believe. Am I equally willing to die for what I believe? Time on earth is brief. What I will be for eternity, however, is being formed now in what, how and why I do what I do. I believe our differences will end in time. That which is good and true in both sides will remain forever in that part of ourselves that transcends time. For that which is common to all men is the quest for what is true, good and beautiful. The intensity of seeking after that in this life is vital if man is ever to fully realize its riches which transcend time and material values. I believe that two men who are earnest in their opposing beliefs, and die in defending them, will develop within themselves the capacity to live in eternal love with one another because the elements of right and wrong on each side will then be fully understood and both will see that if they were sincere they were both struggling to realize the same goals—truth, justice, goodness, happiness and love. All of these are life . . . the eternal characteristic of God.

In the light of these thoughts I decided to carry a weapon. Experience would soon reveal to me something else: that bearing a weapon demanded another kind of courage. For by not carrying a weapon, there was always the chance that in the event your side was captured, things would go better for you. But one fact was clear. If you were bearing a weapon, this made you a combat enemy and you were liable to physical destruction as much as any other soldier. You then had no right to ask for, much less expect to be given, quarter. So, by carrying a weapon you were exposing yourself to yet another door of death.

ten

With Charlie Company at Hoc Mon

It was about the middle of February. The fighting that began so violently at Tet was still widespread. The 5th Mech was in the Hoc Mon area. When I arrived late Sunday afternoon to hold service there I was informed that the troops were occupied in various missions and would not be back until late in the evening. The next morning I hoped to have the service, but the plans were again cancelled when word came that a platoon from Recon, Headquarters Company, was in trouble a few miles away. Charlie Company was to render support, with Bravo Company as back up. Since I was unable to hold the service, I readily accepted the invitation to go along with them. No one at this time thought there would be much trouble. The terrain was open along the way. However, there was something about the atmosphere of the section that seemed threatening. No Vietnamese peasants were seen anywhere. This was usually significant. If the peasants were not committed to the North Vietnamese troops, they normally did not stay around too long in an area where a large force would be building up. A concentrated force meant that a confrontation with government or American forces was close at hand and they did not want to be around when the fireworks began. Usually, if the peasants remained in the area there was a strong likelihood that they were sympathetic with the enemy.

I was on C Company's track with Captain Theologus, the epitome of a professional soldier. He was an intelligent, competent field commander, dedicated, courageous and deeply concerned about the welfare of his men. Accompanying him were his radioman, the artillery forward observer and his radio-man, the driver and the gunner of the track. The track (APC: Army Personnel Carrier) was originally intended to transport troops inside the vehicle. This was unrealistic in this type of war where the terrain lent itself to spider holes from which the enemy could spring up and fire off an RPG rocket into the side of the APC and wipe out everyone inside. So the troops all sat on top of the APC, which was actually safer. If a rocket hit the track you might be blown off, but your chances for survival were better than if you were inside.

At times duds would be dropped by our planes. The enemy would collect them and use them against our troops as mines. Here too, if the mines were not too large there was some chance of survival. The driver, of course, was in a precarious position, since he had to drive the track, and the controls were inside. But GI ingenuity being the way it is, some drivers devised a means to direct their tracks from the top of the vehicle by a set of extended laterals which could attach to the controls inside, thus giving some measure of protection from the mines. Not all mechanized units had this, however. I heard of one newly arrived battalion commander who forbade the use of such attachments. The drivers were to be inside the vehicle, the way the designers planned it. There was a storm of protest raised by the drivers about this, but I never did hear the outcome since I was simply passing by. Such an incident did, however, demon-strate a problem common to the human condition: higher rank-ing people who, because of their position and past experience elsewhere, are reluctant to change established patterns of pro-cedure, although such at times were not pertinent to the exigen-cies of the Vietnamese situation.

Finally reaching our destination we left the main road. It was evident the Recon group was still in trouble. I could not see their position, which seemed to be around the other side of a grove, but could hear some firing, About a hundred meters or so sepa-rated us from that grove of trees. The distance was completely open, offering neither cover nor concealment. The troops were told to hold their positions while the C Company commander and the Bravo Company commander, Captain Stankevitz, surveyed the situation. The Vietnamese interpreter with Charlie Company did not like the looks of the place and began firing across the rice fields to the right of us, checking to see if any snipers might be on our flank. Somewhere inside that grove was an enemy force that was pinning down our Recon group. But there was a large part of that grove on our side which also could contain an enemy force. While attempting to flank the enemy on the far side of the grove, it was also necessary to be cautious in our own assault through this part of the grove. The enemy might be there too.

We discovered a camouflaged hole with a signal lamp in it. This position overlooked the road from which we had just come. It was obviously a spotter's hole. Did this spotter's position have some connection to that grove across the field? As no civilians were noticeable in the area, permission was granted for helicopter gunships to come over and rocket possible sniper positions on our flanks. These gunships then sprayed the grove with light machine gunfire. There was no return of fire. Something was wrong. It seemed too nice and easy. An air strike was requested. A plane soon appeared and dropped about five bombs, half of which turned out to be duds. That was the limit of our air strike. Some artillery was then called in to "prep" the grove for an assault. About a platoon of men had been positioned meanwhile in order to approach the grove on our extreme left flank. With the shelling completed the time had come for the main assault.

Bravo Company would go forward on the right flank. Charlie Company would have some of its men on the left flank, with the remainder moving straight in. The command group was slightly to the right of this frontal action. As we moved across the field, my thought went back several months earlier when I accompanied one of the Mech companies on an Eagle Flight. This Eagle Flight consisted of a group of helicopters moving a company of Mech infantrymen to a predetermined assault area. I recall I felt much the way I was feeling now: the apprehension you have in being aware that you are in the open and approaching a dense area. Was the enemy waiting there in those hedgerows? Closer and closer you came to the dense foliage before you. How many automatic weapons might be trained on your unit at this moment? If the enemy are there, they will get to shoot first. They always do. The beads of sweat matting your forehead are not simply from the heat of the sun. You are afraid. You continue forward with the pressure and strain building up. You wonder what a daily routine like this must do to a man out here month after month. How can they go on? Yet, when the orders are given, "Move out," the troops will go ahead. They may have just returned from hours of searching after the enemy and going through the bitter experience of seeing one of their buddies killed or maimed from enemy mines or booby traps. Instead of rest, they are greeted with the command to load up. An enemy force has been spotted and helicopters will come in ten minutes to move them to the enemy location. They hear the enemy is evidently moving in earnest and they are to be the blocking force. And so their expressionless faces look up to the sky for the copters, and then, saying little, they prepare themselves for the new assault. The heavy extra belts of machine gun ammo are placed crosswise on their chests; the hand grenades are slipped through the straps; extra M16 clips are stuffed in their pockets, while the grenadiers load up with their M79 rounds, and some others carry their claymores for the perimeter defense should they have to dig in for an all night affair. There won't be any hot meal for these troops now. Maybe they can snatch a can of C's while waiting for the copters. And the questions always in the back of their minds: What will they be going into? How bad will it be? They can't be sure. All they can be sure of is that they will be the ones in the "arena."

As I went across the field with these thoughts passing through my mind, I suddenly realized we were just about at the edge of the grove. The command group I was with comprised the CO, his radioman, the artillery observer and his radioman, the interpreter and Tiny, the C Company senior medic. So far, everything was all right. We were inside the grove and the platoon on our far left was well inside it. The physical design of the grove found us just inside the edge of the right side, with a small mound of earth to our left. Then it happened. The unique "snapper-like" sound of the AK 47 was heard just to the left of us. We were being fired upon. Had we been ten feet more to our left on the other side of that mound, we could have been wiped out. We were now warned that the enemy was dug in somewhere to our left. Heavy fire was heard deeper inside the grove in the direction where our left flank was moving. What had happened in the past so many times was happening again. The enemy was well bunkered in and well concealed. The artillery and air strikes did little or no damage. The low lying bunkers were evidently passed over without even being noticed. Now, a group of our men were pinched off inside and we were pinned down in our position.

The first thing was to try and locate exactly where the firing was coming from. Tiny expended his grenades in the general area of fire. Others also opened fire, but it was clear the enemy had excellent cover. The AK 47's kept snapping away at us. We needed assistance if we were to get out of the grove. A tank that had been sent our way as possible support was at a distance. Captain T. rolled out a little from where he was and then exposed himself to catch the tank's attention and direct him to our location. Slowly the tank moved into position and Captain T. pointed out to the tank commander the possible areas where the enemy fire was coming from. Enemy fire increased, but the tankers did a good job and gave us the cover needed to get free.

The captain then assessed the situation. Reports came in that fighting was now heavy along the right flank with Captain Stan's company. Recon was getting some relief as a result of what was going on. It seemed, however, that the left flank was in serious trouble. A few of the group got back to report that they were hit hard. Some men were definitely killed, but they could not be sure how many. One of them thought an RPG rocket struck the platoon leader. They thought that some others of their group were trying to fight their way out of the pocket. Just then several more men of the platoon stumbled towards us. "They were all around us, they were all around us," they kept repeating. The men seemed to be in a state of shock. That they had gotten out at all was a miracle. Everyone was concerned about the rest of the men. Someone then shouted, "Look, there's the platoon leader!" We all looked up and saw him a good distance in the grove. He was dazed and seemed to be mumbling aloud to himself. His movement was very unsteady. He no longer had his weapon. The thought of what he had just been through, the fact of his helpless condition and that he could be cut down at any moment, moved me forward. I wanted to help him.

Nothing else mattered at that moment, although I realized the enemy might be using him as a decoy. A human being was there who needed help. I found myself running into the grove after him. I kept trying to concentrate on his helplessness so as not to panic myself because I was moving into the grove. I recall being surprised that I reached him still untouched and got him to the ground so as to make him less of a target. Almost immediately someone had come up behind me. It was Tiny, the medic. Between the two of us we managed to assist the lieutenant out of the grove. He was in intense pain. The muscles of his shoulder and upper arm were exposed. An RPG fragment had gotten to him. Tiny did a highly competent job in helping the wounded man. A "Dust Off" was summoned and shortly landed. Tiny and I carried the wounded officer on a litter. The lieutenant was very heavy. It was a fatiguing task to carry the wounded man to the copter which had landed in a rice paddy some distance behind us. Especially arduous was getting over the rice berms, which are mounds of dirt serving as a wall to enclose the waters that flood the paddies. These berms are about a foot or two high, but in this place they seemed three feet in places. Trying to lift a two hundred pounder over this while being as gentle as possible was sapping every bit of energy I had. Lifting the litter on to the copter seemed to take every last ounce of strength. When the copter flew off, I recall stumbling to a berm and falling back in complete exhaustion and in such discomfort that for relief I just groaned with every breath.

After a few minutes, I felt better and was able to return to the troops. By this time the track drivers were ordered to move down in a line about seventy meters behind us and train their guns on the grove. Meanwhile, an attempt was made to move back into the grove and remove our men who were still in there. Some progress was made but then the enemy fire grew so intense that our people were forced to fall back. I recall how especially heavy was the RPG rocket fire. It seemed to me that the enemy was firing his rockets at our troops as though they were small arms fire. As the fire fight continued, there was no slackening of this rocket fire. Since our men had been pushed back by the enemy's fire power, more artillery support was requested before our troops would try again to get within the grove. Tired as they were, they wanted to try again.

Two outstanding platoon leaders, Lt. Miller of Charlie Company and Lt. Anderson of Bravo Company, readied their men. Once the shelling by the artillery ended, our troops again made a rush into the grove. This time they entered in far enough to reach one of our men and were able to fight their way out, removing his body from the grove. I recall seeing a wedding band on the dead soldier. While the horror of combat was now over for this young man, what tragic grief would soon come upon his wife and family? Word then reached me that a new medic I had just talked to last week was also killed. I remembered him attending Mass in the field and coming up afterwards and saying he had not bothered to attend service in the States, since the Mass seemed to be said so indifferently by the priests that he considered it blasphemous. You have to possess some love for God to be as sensitive as that young man. He was certainly right. God deserved a better image than the one being given by so many religious "professionals." I was consoled in knowing that this young man could distinguish between the goodness of God and those who were making a mockery of Him. It is not that religion had been tried and failed, but we clergymen and laymen who have failed religion.

Again the fire power of the enemy was increasing. I noticed a number of our M16's on the ground, along with bandoliers of ammunition. These were the weapons of our casualties. I suspected we would be leaving this place by nightfall and the thought of the enemy getting these weapons, ammo and grenades angered me. I made up my mind the enemy would not get his hands on that material. Crawling about, I collected about six or seven rifles and many bandoliers and some grenades. Keeping low, I moved back to an APC and turned them over to the driver there. The thought then occurred to me to take one of the rifles and some ammo and assist our troops. With the casualties they had taken they were clearly in need of some added fire power. Moving forward into different positions, I repeatedly rose up and fired off a number of clips, using the semiautomatic since this afforded greater control and accuracy in shooting into the grove. Then my friend, Jerry West, came over and wanted to use the rifle and clips of ammo. His weapon had jammed. My initial feeling was to tell him to go back to the track where the other rifles had been left, and take one of those. I could see, however, Jerry was concerned for me, so I turned it over to him. As I started back for another rifle, I saw a GI who needed some assistance to reach the evacuation area and so I helped him.

Word was then received that someone was wounded up ahead, and I went forward. As I approached the forward area, I saw Captain T. and Captain Stan ahead with the troops in heavy contact. Captain Stan was waving frantically at me to move out of the open area and come up to their position. The enemy fire was becoming more and more intense, sweeping our right flank with more and more fire power and also giving it to us up front. The situation had taken a turn for the worse. The enemy was apparently on the move to box our small group in. Firing on both sides was now at its highest pitch. The noise was incredible, further augmented by the continuous volleys of the same tank that had helped us earlier. The big gun of the tank set up a great deal of dust and this unexpectedly provided all of us with a smoke screen that enabled our forward group to move back from a fast developing kill zone. After giving some assistance to one of our men, I picked up another of those rifles collected earlier and went back to our new position and started firing again.

My feelings at this time were of deep concern for the troops. They were my people. They were the most important people in the world. I was coming to see something of the phenomenon of love at that moment which was like a revelation. For the first time in my life, I was seeing a comeliness in man that formerly was only so many phrases of beautiful poetry. I felt I was experiencing something wonderfully strong and beautiful in our men. No sacrifice was too much for them to make. They were keenly concerned for the welfare of one another. I felt the presence of the spirit and mystery of the reality of love. We were all one family. White, black, brown—the color of the skin meant nothing. A man's dignity, courage and value were not to be determined by his skin but by what he was as an individual. Paradoxically, in this horror of combat I experienced what was meant by the expression "Man is made in the image and likeness of God." Caught up in a common danger, we saw something of one another that is seldom properly valued and understood today. There is nothing in this world so precious, so good and so beautiful as the human person when he is giving himself for the service of another. In the pain of sacrifice is the metamorphic power of love, transforming man to an ecstatic state of being, which is the realization of God's image.

It was getting dark. Lt. Miller called out to me to stop firing and fall back. We were going to have to leave the area—orders of higher command. We would return early tomorrow. As we pulled back and the men climbed on to the tracks, I saw that Jerry was still with us. So was Captain T. and Tiny. Captain Stan, Lieutenants Miller and Anderson were with their tracks. I sadly saw that many of the tracks did not have as many men returning as started out with us that morning. Morning! It seemed as though the morning was just a few minutes ago. We had actually been engaged for over seven hours.

As the tracks rumbled back to the battalion field position, I looked at the rifle in my hands. Whose rifle was it? Was he wounded or killed? He certainly kept his weapon clean. "Oh, God, please help him. Please strengthen his family."

I was extremely tired. As we moved along the road, I realized we were not back at the battalion area yet. We still had a way to go and it was dark. An ambush was a possibility. I gripped the rifle tightly. A strange awareness was coming over me. I realized that the uniform I was wearing was no longer a costume. I belonged in it for I experienced intimately something of combat. While I always respected deeply the combat soldier, I now reached a new level of appreciation of what was demanded of him.

At the field base camp, we ate a little something and in the darkness held a service. When the Mass was over, one of the GI's present came up and said he and the other soldiers appreciated my being with them that day. Captain T. then offered to let me sleep in his track—a way of Charlie Company saying I belonged.

The next morning, Companies C and B went back to the grove. By now both companies were under strength. The Tet fighting was taking its toll. The tank, therefore, again went with us. I sensed something that made me uncomfortable. I could not put my finger on it, but it boded ill. In the faces of the others, I read my own feelings. No one really wanted to return to that grove. As we approached the area and started off the road, things were quiet. Had the enemy stayed the night? Usually he didn't. This should be but a routine check for bodies. Captain T. decided to send some soldiers to recon the edges of the area where we would be setting up. This turned out to be a salutary decision. The recon group came upon a wounded North Vietnamese soldier whom they captured. Captain T. called a halt of the advancing tracks. The face of that North Vietnamese soldier is still visibly imprinted on my memory. He was young looking and pathetically skinny. His face showed terror at being captured. No doubt he was given some harrowing stories about what happens when captured by Americans, from being skinned alive to being cannibalized. The interpreter found out that he was fighting against us yesterday and was wounded. While he was talking, Tiny dressed his wounds and gave him water from his own canteen. He said his people were still in the grove and that they numbered about four hundred and were waiting for us to return. Now that they knew the fewness of our numbers, they planned to have us get inside the grove and then wipe us out. He said they were well supplied with RPG rockets. While the interpreter was getting this information from the prisoner, Tiny continued to care for him. It was something to see this massive man treating so gently this person who just yesterday was our enemy. Tiny broke open a can of C biscuits and began to feed the prisoner, who seemed confused at the humane treatment he was receiving. The interpreter said he repeated that notion several times in the course of the interrogation.

Captain T. then called back this information to the battalion. Higher command soon came back with a directive for immediate withdrawal from the area. We were to bring the prisoner to battalion field headquarters where G2 (Intelligence) would have a helicopter waiting to take him to Cu Chi for further questioning. We were told the grove would be hit by fighter-bombers shortly and to get out of the area immediately. As the tracks turned around to return to the road, the tank became mired in a steep gully. About five tracks were stranded on the other side of the gully with the enemy positions not too far away. We expected the air attack at any moment and it was supposed to be a heavy one with large bombs. We didn't want to be this close to the grove. With the assistance of some of the tracks, the tank was pulled out and the companies started back with their valuable cargo. Something the prisoner said has never left me. According to him the artillery and gunships did not bother his troops at all when they were dug in. Only the heavy air strikes, namely, the 750 pound bombs and up, caused them any fear. I thought about the routine assault procedure that had been used all during the time I had been in Vietnam up to the present. No wonder so little was effected. For whatever secondary effect the artillery could have had, at least in keeping the enemy with their heads covered, was certainly neutralized by the lack of troop follow up behind the shelling.

As we left that area, many of us kept looking up to the sky for some sign of the bombers. We saw none. It would be three hours before the bombers would arrive. By that time the enemy, seeing our abrupt departure, knew their advantage of surprise no longer existed and that obviously the Americans had something planned for them. Word later came that a large force was seen dispersing from that area. So ended this Hoc Mon incident.

eleven

Since I was out in the field five days each week
and had several Mass services in Cu Chi on Sunday, I found
the responsibility of trying to keep a close watch on the battalion casualties in the hospital difficult. To cover everyone
was impossible with the little time I had. Some of the wounded
might want to speak with me on some important matter while
others might have nothing of moment to discuss. It could happen, therefore, that I wouldn't reach those most in need immediately. It became clear that the hospital portion of my duties
could require all of my time, were I not going out to the field.
To fulfill my responsibilities to the men in the field and also be
of practical assistance to the wounded in the hospital, I decided
not to have my assistant come with me to the forward areas.
Instead of having him assist me there in digging my foxhole,
carrying my gear and setting up my sleeping quarters, I had him
remain at the base camp and check each day on the boys in the
hospital. Wally was to find out who they were, how they were
doing and if they needed something we could provide. Also he
was to inform me if they wished to speak with me on some
private matter. When I came back from the field Wally would
have a list of every one of our people there, exactly what wards
and bed they were in, and any other information I needed about
them. I could then visit those wounded who definitely wanted to
speak with me first, and after seeing them try to cover the rest
of the list with whatever time remained.

In the beginning, Wally was shy about visiting the wounded
whom he didn't know, but when he saw the good he was doing
for those troops, he grew enthusiastic and did an outstanding
job, often going to the PX and spending his own money to

acquire something one of the wounded men requested. Then also Wally would check immediately for the wounded soldiers about any problems with their mail. Being in a hospital bed makes it difficult to communicate with your battalion on some personal matter. The wounded could mention it to the resident hospital chaplain or to the Red Cross girls, but the most they could do was hand on the information through channels. As any serviceman knows, while channels may at times be sure they seldom are swift, especially when you are anxious. As it happened, when news did get to the battalion area about some request from this or that wounded man, whether or not the patient received a response was dependent on the kind of people back at the battalion area. In some company areas of a battalion, there were competent and responsible personnel who would see to the needs of the wounded man. Other companies had "goldbricks" who took their time in responding to the wounded man's request, and in some cases simply disregarded it.

Wally, however, would check with the patients each day. If they had gone through the regular channels and received no word, he would immediately drive our jeep to the company area where he would inform the sergeant about the matter. In some cases Wally would find that the wounded man's request never reached the company area. In other cases, the news reached there, but the individual assigned by the sergeant was simply slow in doing what was requested. In yet other instances, my assistant was given either a run around or bullied by someone pulling rank on him. When I returned from the field, Wally would brief me on the situation and I then would take appropriate action to see that the requests of the wounded were properly considered. I feel that because of Wally's conscientious work, many a wounded GI was spared any further anguish from finding out nobody seemed to care about him once his usefulness was neutralized by his being in a hospital. Such was never the official policy of any battalion or company. However, there are all kinds in so large an organization as the Army and the "duds" can be not only a cause of embarrassment to the command, but in this instance also a source of needless discomfort for those already suffering enough in the hospital.

After being in the field and experiencing combat situations, I found that my visits to certain wards of the hospital sadly depressing as well as terribly frightening. In these wards were the men who recently underwent surgery for gunshot and shrapnel wounds in the stomach or other parts of their body. There were men with one or more of their limbs amputated or without the sight of one or both eyes. The sight of this physical evil was always unnerving. Being out in a combat situation, things are happening so fast that there is little time to think about what could happen. But when I would visit each week these special wards I was vividly reminded of the risks and hideous horrors of combat. Seeing a man with his stomach exposed in plastic, seeing another with tubes protruding all over him, hearing labored breathing and seeing those eyes so pitiful and in such suffering was far worse than seeing the dead. At least you know the dead were no longer suffering physical pain and your faith told you they now have a peace this world certainly did not know, and in the present state of things probably does not even deserve. But for these young wounded men, these sons, fathers or husbands of loved ones back home, a long road of painful recovery lay ahead. For them another kind of battle was to take place, the struggle to surmount their handicaps and achieve a level of life that would contribute to their sense of meaning in society. For some there would be first of all long years of recuperation and then hard years of adjustment.

I wonder if their country appreciates the extreme suffering they bore and the tremendous price they paid in answering the call of their government and not turning away from it. What of those who burned their draft cards and proudly carried about the North Vietnamese flag in the streets of America? Or of those who fled the country rather than serve it? If those people are heroes, as has been declared by some people in this country, then what must these pitiful-looking Americans be who no longer enjoy the use of their precious limbs or sight?

twelve

Much fighting occurred during February and March. By April the allied forces were in control of the situation. The road from Saigon to Tay Ninh was open again and convoys were able to reach their destinations. Charlie Company of the 5th Mech had come upon a very large cache of rice supplies which the enemy had hidden away for his troops. The food was transported to the "Helping Hand" area in Cu Chi. Odds were the food would soon be back in enemy hands since the peasants who would receive the food would be visited by the VC sometime at night to demand the rice as a "tax" payment. Since Captain T. knew some orphanages in Cholon who could certainly use such food and where enemy extortion was less likely, the company commander made arrangements with his superiors to bring a truck load to these orphanages during his company's next stand-down in Cu Chi.

The opportunity for this goodwill mission came in April. The captain had no problem finding volunteers for this mission. American troops in general are generous. This would be but another example of that generosity.

The first step was to go over to the "Helping Hand" area and load the truck. The volunteers, about ten of them, worked with great gusto in loading on the large sacks of rice. It was satisfying to know that at least some of the captured rice wasn't going back to the enemy. Once the allotted supply of rice was on the truck, it was noticed that there was still substantial room left. Close by were carton upon carton of powdered milk, eggs and oat cereal. The troops agreed that the babies in the orphanage could certainly find use for this and so I was chosen to speak with the yard manager about the possibility of taking some of these food stuffs. Our acquisition slip didn't have these food items listed. What then took place was like a comedy scene from the silent movies era. I approached the sergeant and began telling him about the orphanage and the little babies there, how much they needed substantial food like milk, eggs and oat cereal, and since he had so much of those items on hand, would he let us have some? As the sergeant faced me his back was to the troops and the truck.

It just so happened that those food items in question were also within reach of the troops. While the sergeant was replying that he could well sympathize with our cause but that nonetheless he had a standard operating procedure which had to be followed, etc., etc., I could see the troops behind him working feverishly loading the truck with the cartons of milk, eggs and cereal. The troops were working so fast and so quietly that it looked like an old time movie flick. No sound, just fast quiet action. I realized now why I was selected as the spokesman. The troops were using me as a decoy to keep the attention of the enemy (who in this case was an unsuspecting sergeant) while they tactically placed themselves in a maneuverable position and pulled what I will always remember as the Cu Chi caper. At this point I found myself in a perplexing situation. If I stopped talking, the sergeant might turn around and catch the scene (a real steal) going on behind him. His dedication to the rules was obvious, and I feared the confrontation of his dedication and the troops' exuberance. The troops had just returned from months of hard fighting and the thought of bringing milk, eggs and cereal to little babies was a refreshing change from what they had been doing. I decided to keep right on talking to avoid the impact of that irresistible force meeting this immovable barrier.

With the rice and other food items nicely stashed (I suppose that's the appropriate word under the circumstances!) in the truck, we lined up with the other vehicles going by convoy that day to the Saigon area. After the usual Army routine of "hurry up and wait," we finally were on our way. The trip along the highway was uneventful, a pleasant change. The convoy route ended at Tan Son Nhut, which contained a large airbase, and many military buildings of ours and of the South Vietnamese. A training area for South Vietnamese Rangers was also there. The Tan Son Nhut complex was large and the numerous American military personnel with their clean uniforms and polished boots suggested that being here was a lot like being in "the world." There were paved streets with sidewalks, so unlike Cu Chi with its dirty, dusty roads which had to be often covered with a smelly crude oil product to keep down the dust. We passed a covered outdoor gym where some military personnel were working up a healthy sweat from their game of basketball. We saw tennis courts where the military net set were having at it. The people on the streets looked so neat and clean that I began to feel ashamed, as though I didn't belong there. No one carried weapons. There obviously was no need. A number of the military offices showed air conditioners protruding from the windows. I started scanning about for some swimming pools to make the picture of home complete. To think, all this plus sixty-five dollars a month extra as combat pay. I looked at our tired, grimy combat troops. They also received sixty-five dollars a month extra combat pay, for working out of Cu Chi. What a difference just twenty or so miles can make!

We soon passed through Tan Son Nhut and entered Saigon. I was surprised to see how large a city Saigon was. But what especially impressed me was that the city people gave no indication a war was going on. As we drove through the city it seemed we could just as well have been driving through almost any large, overcrowded city in the States. People, people, people all over, scurrying here and there. Some on motorbikes, some in tiny cars, some on bicycles and others being transported by rickshaw. As always, there were those overcrowded, cartoon-like Vespa busses with their sea of heads and sardine-packed bodies inviting such a caption as "Anybody driving?" Occasionally a military vehicle would be seen moving about. I recall the city as noisy and terribly dirty. One avenue showed some large homes of the wealthy, but most of the streets had tiny, corrugated, box-like structures which served as houses for the poor.

The movement of traffic on a Saigon street is something to behold. With the exception of an area near the government palace, there did not appear to be any red lights to keep a semblance of order in the traffic. Instead, when you approached an intersection, it was simply a matter of how much "nerve" you had to go bulldozing your way through and not deviate from your determined course. It seemed as though everyone was equally determined not to so deviate and the result was one long series of suspenseful experiences as you approached successive intersections. What fascinated me was that no one crashed into anyone else. This was astounding. After a few intersections I became accustomed to what was happening and then broke into almost uncontrollable laughter. What a sight: impassive, fatalistic-looking faces of the Vietnamese moving seemingly in all directions at once and slim Viet girls riding sidesaddle on the back of the bikes of their boyfriends or husbands. These girls were beautifully and neatly dressed and showed no concern whatsoever that only inches were separating them from what would have been fantastic pileups. These motorbikes were really moving. As I write about this, I find I am still awed as ever at that remarkable exhibition of chaotic traffic, noisy streets, colorful costumes and polluted air. What a scene!

Soon I noticed a difference in the city. Instead of store and shop signs being printed in Vietnamese they now appeared to be in Chinese script. We were entering the Chinese section of the city known as Cholon. In about a month from now parts of this district would be hit hard by the VC and North Vietnamese. At this time there were no significant problems here. The Chinese are industrious and almost everywhere you saw shops of one kind or another. We then turned down a tiny street and came upon the first of the orphanages we would be visiting that day. Our boys received a warm welcome and with little children looking on, and some of the bigger ones trying to help, the food items were unloaded from the truck. The faces of our troops showed keen delight in what was being done. None of them seemed to notice the heat, so taken were they by the enthusiasm and friendliness of the little orphans.

After the unloading we had a chance to go through the small orphanage which was neat and clean. I learned that few of the orphan children were of Viet and American parentage. The percentage was about one percent.

Some of the children were left by Viets who simply could not care for them. Others were simply left there for a while until the parents could make a proper home for the child. There were those, both of whose parents were killed by the ravages of war. The reasons for children becoming orphans are never pleasant. It was consoling to know there were dedicated people in this world who cared enough about these young innocent lives to try to help them at a time when they were certainly most helpless. The people working at the orphanage showed deep warmth for all the children who were forever craving after signs of affection and love. Some of these children would be adopted. These were perhaps more fortunate than many children who had never known the poor halls of an orphanage. For the adopted child knows that he or she is wanted, and wasn't simply the result of an unwanted accident on the part of the parents. Many of these orphans, however, never would be adopted. It was comforting to us that at least in this orphanage there would be same memories of love they could forever take with them when the day arrived for them to go out and make their own life.

After a refreshing drink, of cool lemonade we set out for the other orphanage which turned out to be small and located in a depressing slum area. As the building was away from the road we had to take a circuitous route to reach it. The only dirt road available was extremely narrow with a drainage trench only inches from the left wheel of the massive five ton truck. There were some tense moments when Captain T. walked the vehicle through that area. The prospects of a five ton truck disabled in a trench would not sit well with our superiors. The driver kept cool and following the directions of Captain T. brought his vehicle through that area.

When we arrived at the orphanage we again were greeted with great warmth and friendliness, although I noticed there was much less material comfort here than at the last orphanage where there was little enough. The troops soon had what remained in the truck unloaded. Shortly after, we departed behind the spirited shouting and grateful waving of the children and adults at the orphanage.

With the food having been delivered, the troops set off for Cu Chi. We would follow behind in the jeep, but first there was another matter. For several months, one of the GI's in Captain T.'s company had expressed a desire to initiate proceedings for the adoption of a Vietnamese child. Since we were in Saigon the captain decided to bring the GI to the U.S. embassy for information. There the GI was directed to speak with a certain private adoption agency approved by the Saigon government. We were told the agency was open and we should go over there. This we did.

Upon arrival I waited in the jeep while the GI, accompanied by Captain T. and Sgt. Long, the Vietnamese interpreter for Charlie Company, went to the door of the agency. They knocked for some time before the door was finally opened. Some kind of conversation went on and then the door was closed with the three of them still standing outside. As they walked back to the jeep, their faces told me things did not go well.

I found out that although the woman who was in charge was there, she would not see them since it was after office hours. She told them to come tomorrow. I thought that was understandable. She probably thinks our people are stationed in Saigon, but surely when she knows the nature of our situation she will make an exception and grant us a few moments of her time. I mentioned this to the others. So all of us returned there and after a while the door again opened. I requested permission for us to enter. Reluctantly, it was given. Once inside, I explained the predicament of the soldier: that he had been in the field for some time; that he had come with us today to assist in bringing food to two orphanages in the Cholon area; that he would have to return to his unit today for more field duty and that he would appreciate receiving some information on what would be required by the agency for adoption proceedings. The woman in charge was adamant in her refusal to be in any way cooperative. "Come back tomorrow," was her reply. I then pleaded with her to make an exception for the sake of this gentleman who would not be able to come tomorrow and could not be sure when he would have the opportunity to visit Saigon in the immediate future. "Come back tomorrow," she said. "Couldn't you at least give him some printed information he could read?" I asked. "We are closed. Come back tomorrow," she said. "Is this all the consideration you can give this American who has such concern and respect for your people?" I queried. With this, the woman gave a disdainful smile. No matter how much I pleaded and begged, she would not move from her position. We finally left, not only disappointed but feeling the needling stings of disillusionment.

That day provided a contrast. The generous, friendly giving of our people of what we had to give and the refusal on the part of one of their people of what could have been given. Technically the woman was right. I assume it was after office hours. I can see that in the past, this woman could have met gauche Americans who may have lorded over the woman the fact that America was spending billions of dollars for the Vietnamese, as if implying there was something second-rate about her people. Perhaps she felt some deep resentment that the Americans were in her country at all. If the Americans were never here, her country's orphanages would not have been as full. I do not know what was going on in her mind. It may have had to do with what I mentioned above. Then again, she might have simply represented that kind of agency worker who unfortunately can be found anywhere in the world—the kind of person who does just what is required, although the nature of the agency is deeply involved in humane matters. I recall two Red Cross workers. One was thoroughly dedicated to the mission of the agency, and so not simply an employee of some business. People were always her primary concern, even if it meant her working past the closing hour. The other Red Cross worker was the opposite. His main concern was to do the minimum required for his check. He didn't care about the needs of people. Such agency workers as this are an anomaly to the nature of the agency for which they work. Perhaps that Vietnamese agency worker was of the latter mold, but the four of us who were in that office that day were there out of friendship and love of the Vietnamese people. Not to receive any consideration nor understanding for our predicament from that Vietnamese agency worker meant to us the feelings were not mutual. This is what was so painful to us. It was now late in the afternoon. We would have to move fast to reach Cu Chi before nightfall.

thirteen

It was evening when I was called by my assistant to report to the executive officer at headquarters. I had just crawled into my bunker, arranged the mosquito netting and was beginning to relax and make plans for the coming field trips to the Wolfhounds. I didn't realize how tired my body was until I tried to move out of the bunker. Riding in a jeep over rough roads was not helping my back problems. I finally worked my way outside and started for headquarters. "What's going on, Wally?" "I don't know for sure, but it seems some new replacement is inside one of the troop's bunkers and is threatening to commit suicide. He has a rifle and won't let anyone into the bunker. He says he'll shoot anybody who tries to enter." As usual Wally had all the information, for when I arrived at headquarters that's what the situation was. I was asked to talk to the soldier. Several others had tried but no one had been able to get inside the bunker.

As I walked to the bunker, I wondered how psychologically disturbed this boy might be. The thought of being shot at any time is never pleasant, but to be shot by your own is doubly obnoxious. I inquired into the background of the soldier. Were his parents alive? Did he profess any religion? Did he have a girl friend or wife? That last information proved to be critical.

When I arrived at the bunker a lieutenant and an enlisted man were standing along the side of the entrance. They had been talking to the soldier inside. Their caution signaled the evident unpredictability of the young man inside the bunker. I called him by his first name, telling him I was the chaplain of the battalion. As he had just come to the battalion he had never seen me, but the notion of a "chaplain" as someone sincerely interested in the welfare of the soldier should remain from his experiences in basic training back in the States. I told him I would like to come in and talk with him and that it was difficult to try and hold a conversation with both of us where we were. He said to stay away or he would shoot. The things he then said indicated he was ashamed of being afraid to go out to the field. I reminded him that fear is common to all of us. Then I said something that caught his interest. I called out the name of his wife and asked, "Do you think Joan would be pleased with the way you are acting? Have you thought about that?" He immediately responded, "How did you know about Joan?" I told him I knew and that I would like to talk to him about her, but that we could not have a very private conversation shouting back at one another with other people all around. "Would you let me come in to speak with you?" I asked. "You're trying to trick me," he yelled in an aggravated tone. "No, I'm not. Please trust me," I responded. "You're trying to trick me," he repeated, now in a threatening tone. As he was becoming excited, I mentioned his wife's name several times while speaking to try and calm him down. Then, I said, "If you love your wife, you will let me come in and talk with you . . . I believe you do love your wife and that she has something to do with why you are acting the way you are . . . I am going to stand in front of the entrance. The light is behind me. It's dark where you are. You will be able to see me but I won't be able to see you. I am putting my life in your hands." I stood in the entrance way. I was counting heavily that my suspicions about his wife's part in this present situation held the key to his present actions. So there I was, staring into pitch-blackness, with the light behind me, a helpless target if he were seriously ill.

No shot rang out. I began to slowly grope my way through the darkness. The bunker had wooden slats for the floor and heavy beams to support the roof which was covered over with sandbags. There was the usual musty smell of such places. Little by little my eyes became accustomed to the darkness.

Finally I saw a figure huddled at one corner of the bunker. As I approached he suddenly stopped pointing the rifle at me and placed the muzzle under his chin, warning me not to try to take the rifle from him or he would shoot himself. I told him I had no intention to trick him, much less hurt him. I asked if I could sit next to him. He nodded, indicating "yes." His eyes appeared to be popping from their sockets. I started speaking to him and soon found out that he was terrified at going out to the field. Being a medic, he was aware of what was expected of them. He earlier thought he could go through with it, but when he arrived at Cu Chi something happened. He couldn't go out to the field. Because of that he felt ashamed. He was failing his buddies, but mostly he felt he was bringing shame on his wife. How could she ever be proud of him? But if he went out to the field and was killed, he would lose her, and this was an unbearable thought. His mind was in a dilemma. Suicide seemed the only answer. Yet suicide would also mean being separated from his wife. He was confused, frightened, and in the throes of genuine anguish.

I tried to explain to him that medics also served in the hospital. He should spend some time working as a medic there, serving the soldiers who were wounded. He was reminded that he would be performing an important service to men who needed him there and that perhaps in time by being with them and helping them, he might see things differently. It is amazing how deeply a bond can develop when you are associating with combat troops. There is something beautiful about them in their simplicity, quiet courage and sense of loyalty and concern for one another. I have known where this bond has grown so deep that even when offered a safer job, the soldier would prefer to remain with his buddies. So I told this young soldier to give himself a chance to grow and to give his wife a chance to be proud of him. He seemed to show some interest in this but didn't believe anything could be done. At this point, a voice called in to us. It was that of the executive officer of the battalion. He asked if he too could come in. When I asked the soldier, he agreed. This officer was a fine man with a deep sensitivity for the needs of his troops. When he was informed of the circumstances he said he would see to it that this soldier would be assigned to the hospital. The young man looked at both of us incredulously. The officer then asked him to turn his rifle over to me. There was a moment of hesitation and then he took the rifle away from his chin and gave it to me. I nodded encouragingly to the young soldier, then the three of us left the bunker. A later examination of his rifle showed he did have a shell in the chamber. All he had to do was pull the trigger. As it was, he didn't and everyone was thankful.

fourteen

The morale of the troops is of primary importance. Whatever may undermine this morale does jeopardy not only to the mission of the Army, but fundamentally threatens the well-being of the troops. When a combat soldier becomes despondent, he can become dangerous to himself and to everyone around him.

The reception of a "Dear John" letter is an example of what often posed a serious problem. Such a letter might be received by one of our servicemen while serving in Vietnam. This letter informed the GI in question that he was no longer the center of his girl's affection and that someone else in the States had taken his place. In some cases the letters had to do with the wife wanting a divorce or a fiancée wishing to break her engagement. In almost every letter that was ever shown me there would be a statement to the effect that this "news" was being sent the GI so as not to hurt him. I assume there was no malice in such a statement, but it reeked with insensitivity. If there is one thing a GI needs when in the hardships of combat, it is something to live for, something to motivate him to perform his duties effectively no matter how boring or dangerous. Deprive him of that motivating force and you may well rob him of an intangible without which he may jeopardize himself and those around him. I know of several instances when men who had received the "Dear John" letters were killed soon after. Their friends told me that they had become so depressed by that letter that they could not keep their minds on what they were doing, where they were, and the dangers involved. It seemed far more humane to wait until the man returned from Vietnam before informing him of such changes. I am aware of two cases where this information was withheld until their arrival back home. Granted this was a shock, but there were far more distractions back in the States than out in the field to recuperate from such a bitter disappointment.

When men had me read their "Dear John" letter, I'd try to help them face up to the reality before them. Love is no game. It is deeply serious, a mystery which demands respect. You cannot force anyone to love you. Love must be spontaneous. You may love someone, but that does not necessarily create love for you in the other person. In all human love there is selfishness. However, when that selfishness enlarges to the point where the happiness of the other is secondary to your own, then the genuineness of such love is suspect. Further, if a person who said they loved you when you were in their presence lost that love when you were no longer physically present, such would be a superficial type of love you could well do without. Some of the men listened and discovered something about themselves by the way they were reacting. Others refused to listen, to the detriment of themselves and those about them.

Another area pertinent to morale centered around certain problems at home which could cripple a soldier's effectiveness in the fulfillment of his duties in Vietnam. I recall the case of a sergeant who was competent and highly respected by everyone in the battalion. One day he came to me upset and had me read his wife's letter. The letter told of how she had been attacked many months earlier and how the man responsible was still coming to her apartment and threatening the children should she contact the police. Since he lived in the apartment downstairs she was in continual fear of his presence. Now she has found she is pregnant. She begged her husband to forgive her, but she did not know what to do. She feared for the safety of the children. It happened the sergeant knew this man since he owned the apartment house in which the sergeant's wife and children were living while he was in Vietnam.

The sergeant had been in Vietnam ten months. He told me he was no longer able to perform his duties. The thought of his wife and the danger to his family simply overwhelmed him. Seeing such an outstanding man as this so broken up convinced me he should be returned to the States as quickly as possible. We brought the matter up with the executive officer, and he too was of the opinion the sergeant should return home and he so informed the commanding officer of the situation. While not enthused at losing so competent a man, the CO appreciated the serious nature of the problem and recommended approval for a compassionate transfer to the States. With swift verification by the Red Cross of the pertinent circumstances, the documents for compassionate transfer were quickly assembled and in the hands of higher headquarters. They, however, were reluctant to approve this request on the grounds that this was probably a clever ruse on the part of the sergeant to acquire an early out from Vietnam. When the sergeant informed me of this he was almost incoherent, so emotionally overwrought was he. I then presented myself to a representative of higher headquarters and reminded that person he was overriding recommendations from the CO of the battalion, the executive officer, the company commander, the Red Cross and myself. I made it clear that if any harm came to that sergeant through an emotional breakdown, I would reveal to the highest authorities this representative's unreasonableness and insensitivity to the sergeant's urgent request and recommend that this representative be held responsible for whatever consequences might result. The next day, as I was preparing to go out to the field, the sergeant came to me and said his transfer had been approved.

It wasn't long after that another serious case came to my attention. A young soldier showed me a number of letters from his wife. He was alarmed by their tone. He said his wife was highly emotional but that his presence had always been a stabilizing influence, Now that he was away her letters seemed to show a deterioration of the mind taking place. In studying the letters, I saw that the wife would start on one subject, and then in the same sentence break off from that train of thought and discuss something else completely out of context. She would begin questions but before finishing them she would go off into rapturous descriptions of her fantasies and then just as quickly return to a train of thought begun earlier. I requested the Red Cross to investigate this. As a result of their subsequent investigation, the young man was granted a compassionate transfer.

In general, I was impressed with the willingness of the Army to try and assist its needy personnel when it was at all possible. In that part of its design to cover the emergency problems of its personnel, the Army is a remarkable organization. If any criticism is to be launched against the Army in this area, it should be directed against those individuals whose duty it is to carry out this design, but who through incompetence or gross negligence betray this function.

fifteen

The monsoon season was upon us. Usually certain times each day we would have showers. This afternoon, however, while I was on my way out to the Wolfhounds, the usual showers did not make their appearance. That meant the evening downpour would truly be torrential. Our convoy arrived at the field base camp around fifteen hundred hours in the afternoon. Since one of the line companies happened to be in camp that day, I decided to hold a service for them then, just in case the service in the evening for the remainder of the battalion should be rained out. By the time I finished the service and spoke with some of the troops on personal matters, it was chow time. The rest of the troops were now back in camp and I planned on holding service for them after they had eaten. Before the scheduled time, however, tremendous black clouds began moving our way. I had no chance thus far to set up my lean-to. Now, the clouds were moving in fast. Deep rumblings of thunder only made the scene more ominous. I put both my service kit and gear under a large canvas where some electronic supplies were kept. The troops were scurrying to their lean-tos. Some GI's invited me to crowd in with them under their five man lean-to. But there were already five men there, and I didn't want to have anyone getting soaked because of me. I told them I'd be all right and that I'd find some shelter elsewhere. By now the wind was blowing strongly. Thunder made the artillery's eight inch guns sound like children's toys. Throwing on my poncho, I went off looking for shelter. By now the rains were sweeping in. I came upon the jagged wreckage of a war-torn cottage. The roof was no longer there. A large disabled cart leaned next to one of the walls still remaining upright. That would be my shelter. For over an hour the rain came down in torrents, with the wind unmercifully blowing it every which way. I could hear the shell-scarred cottage wall straining behind me. The cart seemed at times as though it too would collapse under the relentless pounding of the storm. The rain would let up for a while and then I would hear a weird wailing sound as the wind plaintively caressed the tragic remains of the cottage. Where are the people who once lived here, I wondered. I felt sad, with a sense of loneliness coming over me. Then the rains again increased and soon reached such an intensity that the various troop lean-tos and bunker positions were no longer visible. The thought occurred to me that anyone could enter the battalion base camp at this time with little chance of being challenged. I fervently hoped the enemy were not moving in our direction. Under these circumstances there would be nothing but disastrous confusion.

As the rain again slackened I started thinking about our troops, the kind of people they were, the motivation they were supposed to have in carrying out their duties and the degree to which they actually fulfilled their responsibilities. As in most instances where a human dimension is involved, there would be plus and negative signs.

On the plus side, they certainly manifested courage in the face of trying situations. Living under combat field conditions has its own peculiar hardships. Often the troops have to trudge long hours in the heat of the sun and then with little or no rest move out again in the evening. They have to spend chilly nights on ambush, lying in mud or ditches filled with stagnant water. They have to live with the threat of an enemy attack at any time, while finding themselves in the awkward position of being unreasonably restricted as to where and when they may defend themselves. For, "recon by fire," a tactical means which would limit the enemy's advantage of ambush, was often denied our troops, since many of the areas they went through had been stipulated as "non-fire zones" or "restricted areas" where permission had to be obtained ahead of time before any firing could take place. Thus the enemy were given the advantage of killing and maiming our troops in situations that would have occurred less often if our troops had not been so restricted. I have heard of people decrying the immorality of this war from the viewpoint of what it was doing to civilians. As of this writing I have not heard anyone decry the immorality of clothing a man with a military uniform, giving him a rifle, placing him in a hostile surrounding and then restricting the use of the means he has to defend himself. Considering how the government has treated them like expendables, and has shown more concern about negative world opinion, be it communist or otherwise, than about the defensive welfare of its troops, I'd say the biggest positive sign for our men in uniform was the miracle that they were in this hostile foreign country at all! That these men did not burn their draft cards, did not run away from their country and did not refuse to enter the service is indicative of a loyalty and respect for their government which does not seem to be matched by that government or the country it is supposed to represent. In this sense the courage of our troops is indeed remarkable.

On the negative side, I observed in many of our troops a kind of wanton carelessness in how they functioned. Unnecessary casualties would mount because of apparent disregard for proper security procedures. Men would be killed or maimed from short rounds fired by mortar or artillery. Regulations about the size and arrangement of an ammunition dump would be violated with disastrous results to men and matériel. Random rounds of ammo would be thoughtlessly thrown into sump holes. Later the refuse in the hole would be lighted with the ammo firing off, exposing people to injury. Any dynamiting to be done in a field area was supposed to be made known well in advance of the "Fire in the Hole!" warning. At times, the yell "Fire in the Hole!" was almost simultaneous with the explosion going off, giving no time for anyone to take proper cover. Often when I would walk around the perimeters of our field area I would find bunkers unattended, with hand grenades, ammo and claymore mines just waiting to be picked up by the children of the near-by villages. Ultimately this would fall into the hands of the VC to be used as booby traps against our troops.

In moving out from one field position to another, some would leave ammo behind so as not to be bothered packing it. Once the American troops would leave an area the Vietnamese would come in and pick the place clean, digging up even the sump holes. VC could scavenge as well as anyone else. Radio batteries, when the stipulated number of hours was reached, were often simply discarded instead of being destroyed. Some communications people showed me where there was enough juice left in those discarded batteries to light a bulb of substantial wattage for a number of hours. The VC could take such a battery and use it to set off various types of mines. A demolition team member told me silver foil from gum wrappers could be used by the enemy as terminal conductors for a mine. Yet such wrappers would often be carelessly thrown aside.

A company of tracks leave the base camp on a mission. Another company of troops are assigned to guard the perimeter and immediate area. Boom Boom girls (prostitutes) come and distract the troops and while this is going on the VC are setting mines right outside the perimeter where the tracks will be moving on their return. The result: a track is blown and an excellent commander is injured. A battery of 155's has with it troops for security. Boom Boom girls make their appearance by prearranged plan at night and while the security is busy with them the VC come in and destroy a number of the large self-propelled guns. A commanding officer speaks to his troops and tells them how hard he was trying to keep them alive and how difficult they were making it for him by their carelessness. Five soldiers are in a combat outpost. All five go to sleep and so no one is found watching the assigned sector. The enemy come up, slit their throats, then move in and fire their rockets at the battalion area, killing some and wounding many more. I recall another incident when a company was making its way through a thick growth near a river. The CO had told them not to talk. Yet they were so noisy in their chatter that the company field area knew they were on their way in long before they were visually seen. There was another incident along a canal when I was with some troops. We heard a small boat coming in our direction. We hid in the brush as it went by. There in the boat were several GI's all talking loudly with their weapons nowhere in sight. None of them were looking to the right or left. They were inviting an ambush. Later just such a boat was ambushed with dire results.

These forms of carelessness by some of our troops along with an increasing use of marijuana or pot among them indicated an alarming lack of moral discipline. Where does one look for the possible source of this problem? Is this carelessness a sign of a lack of toughness, not only physical, but especially moral, as shown by the rampant use of drugs to get away from it all? Sergeants have told me how the system of troop training today is not as rugged as it was in the past. Their hands are tied by irate mothers writing their congressmen about alleged inhumane treatment of their sons by the Army. Although there is such a thing as excessive harassment which is harmful, there is nonetheless value in reasonable harassment. It develops in a soldier a patience and an endurance for what is unpleasant and thus helps him to be better able to perform his duties despite the monotony or pressures before him. When later he finds himself out in the field faced with the many discouraging unpleasantries there, he is better equipped to cope with them. He is better able to face up to the harsh exigencies of his situation instead of pretending they weren't really there. He can live with what is obnoxious and not look for compensations such as pot, or openly disregarding security regulations as a deceptive way to lessen the mental anguish that comes from being aware that one's situation is indeed dangerous or uncomfortable.

The answer to the problem of moral discipline, however, goes deeper than this. Men may wear uniforms, but what the uniform stands for will be more or less realized by what is inside it. And what is inside it has come from a given environment. What is the moral environment this man has come from? Is he a morally tough person? What are his values? What is his attitude to law, to justice, and to his responsibilities as a man? Does he believe in principles? What kind of example has he been given since he was born? From his parents? From his teachers and friends? What kind of example has been shown him by local, state, and government officials? What have the doctors and church people shown him as to the dignity of the human person? To what extent has the double standard as exercised by those in high positions negatively affected him? Do our youth find in their leaders at all levels a source of inspiration, instilling in them by their example a willingness to make sacrifices, to be altruistic and to believe there is such a thing as unselfish service to others? Or have they become confused and cynical because of what they see as contrasted to what they have heard?

The effects of a lack of moral discipline which I observed while in Vietnam were, I believe, a symptomatic representation of a general moral weakness unfortunately infecting the inner structure of our American society today.

sixteen

A Dangerous Time

It was now May, and the North Vietnamese and VC had launched the second phase of their Tet Offensive. The goal of the enemy was again Saigon. Reports were being circulated that the enemy was actually in certain portions of Cholon. I hoped those portions did not include the orphanages. As I was unable to acquire any definite information, I decided I would go into the Cholon area and see for myself and bring some food along at the same time. The mess sergeants cooperated with whatever extra food they could spare, and soon a ¾ ton truck was filled. As Wally, my assistant, did not have a military license for trucks, I had to locate a volunteer. Before long, a young GI, by the name of Coverdale, from Charlie Company, offered to do the driving. He was now a short-timer, no longer out in the field, but working now in the comparative safety of Cu Chi in the convoy. Knowing this, he nonetheless still wanted to make the trip.

This operation was much smaller than the one with Captain T. Before, we had a sizable number of troops with us, but now there was only the three of us in this ¾ ton. I had Wally sit up front with Coverdale and ride as shotgun. I sat on top of the food boxes in the back of the truck and did the same.

On our way to Saigon, there were several delays along the road because of various troop movements. When we arrived at Saigon, I again was amazed to find everything much like it was on the last trip with Captain T. If there was a war going on, you would never know it. On entering Cholon things seemed normal for awhile there too, but as we continued towards our destination, the streets were suddenly empty. The shops were all closed. There was something wrong; we could feel it. Soon we made a turn down a small street only a few blocks from the orphanage. It was hard to believe this was the same section we passed by just a few weeks earlier. Building after building was rubble. I feared for the orphanage. Would it be there? What about its occupants? I took a deep breath as we turned the corner. Thank God! It was still there. The street, however, was empty.

When we reached the building, I left the ¾ ton and banged on the door. The sound of heavy metal echoed through the courtyard within. No one answered. I knocked again. While waiting I noticed bullet marks all along the walls of the building. At that moment there were footsteps on the other side. The peep latch opened and a pair of frightened eyes looked at me. Once recognizing who I was, the director of the orphanage spoke apprehensively, "You have come at a very dangerous time, Chaplain!" She quickly unbolted the door to let me in. I told her we brought some food. Her face told me we were in answer to prayer, for marketing had been impossible for some time.

The larger metal doors were then opened and the driver did a fine job of backing in the vehicle. Another coat of paint on that ¾ ton and he would never have made it. The metal doors were again closed. Once inside the truck was quickly unloaded. The faces of the older children showed great fear, and with good reason, for now a sound familiar to all of us—that of the mortar—was heard. The mortars were dropping only a few meters down the street. We rushed inside the building where the director filled me in on the fighting that was going on all around them. I could now hear the snap of the AK-47's. The enemy were definitely in the area. The director suggested we get away. She feared for our lives. I mentioned my concerns for all in the orphanage. She seemed deeply appreciative and then said, "Our children are in the hands of God."

By now the intensity of the firing down the street had given way to sporadic bursts. I went up to the second floor and peered out a window. I could see government troops cautiously moving along the sides of the houses on the street toward the direction of the fire. I felt better about the safety of the orphanage personnel when I saw they were obviously pushing the enemy away. In conscience I felt we then could leave. I told the driver to wait for my signal.

After checking the street and corner, I summoned the driver to drive the truck out of the courtyard. The large metal gate closed behind him. I could see a hand waving from behind the peep latch. I waved back. Once on the truck, the driver opened up and we soon were out of the Cholon area.

We were now driving through Saigon. No longer were the streets bare nor the buildings rubble-strewn. People were running about here and there on their motorbikes. Shopkeepers were busy selling their wares. It was as though we had just emerged from a time machine into another world. Such is the incredible phenomenon of war in South Vietnam.

seventeen

With so much enemy action concentrating on Saigon almost all the companies of our battalions were operating blocking actions around that city. Because our combat troops were relatively close to Saigon, the higher command decided there was no need to send supplies all the way to Cu Chi. The battalion supply trains would now be located along the wire at the Tan Son Nhut airfield. It would be from there that field troops would now be supplied.

Formerly when our troops had been supplied from Cu Chi I could reach the field by the supply Chinook or by the battalion convoy. Now, with the supply trains of each battalion away from Cu Chi, I had first to reach the general supply area at the airfield before I had any chance of being transported to the field. That meant I would first have to travel by convoy from Cu Chi to the airfield near Saigon. The route of this convoy was like a testing run dreamed up by sadistic engineers to put the company's trucks to their breaking point. Bouncing about in the back of a five ton Army truck was always a grueling experience. It was impossible to sit for any length of time on the wooden bench since your body would be lifted from the seat by the bumps in the road and then jarred violently as your buttocks smashed back upon the splinter filled bench. Knocked now this way, now that way, you soon found it necessary to stand upright to obtain some relief. But this too offered problems, for if you stood up too straight you could easily be catapulted right out of the speeding truck. After about forty minutes of this you arrived at the airfield feeling much the same way you did after a full week out in the field, only now you were just getting started.

Once at the airfield I slowly made my way to the headquarters of one of the battalion supply trains. There I requested to go on their next supply run to the field. Sometimes this meant going by Chinook, at other times by convoy. Since it was much cheaper to supply by convoy than by Chinook, the convoy would be used whenever feasible. A typical Wolfhound convoy would consist of a lead jeep with a light machine gun mounted in the back. Manning this weapon was a GI with a pet monkey on his shoulder. This cigar-chewing soldier with his handlebar mustache made an unforgettable picture. Then would follow the supply officer's jeep, driven by a "speedy 4" (a GI specialist, 4th class). Usually I was squeezed in the back part of this jeep with some sergeant or officer also going out to the field. When it was crowded there, I would sit on the back fender guard. Behind this jeep there would be different company trucks with the evening meal for the troops and other supplies and troops. Behind the last truck there was usually a rear guard jeep.

During the dry season the roads were covered by an inch or so of powdery dirt which was quickly churned up by the movement of the convoy. Soon the line of vehicles looked like a massive cloud of yellowish-brown dust ploughing along the road. By the time you reached the field position, you were caked over with this dust. Your mouth, nostrils and throat were coated with this powdery dirt. Your eyes would sting if you weren't wearing goggles to protect them. You would be intensely thirsty, but when you would put the tepid water from your canteen to your lips, you would experience the foul taste of the dirt particles which would soon make you nauseous. During the wet season, however, you would be spared these inconveniences and so would find the trip less discomforting.

Aside from discomfort, the convoy trips could be interesting, especially when you would pass through villages off the main roads. It was like another world. The thorn in the pillow, however, was the possibility of running into an ambush or being mined. I recall being with another battalion convoy when the truck up ahead was obviously hit by a command detonated mine. This is the type of mine that is controlled by someone in the vicinity. In this way the enemy can hit the vehicle he wants, and not have to settle for whatever first comes over the mine. Anyone can set a mine such as this off, including a young child or old woman.

There was also the possibility of snipers but I recall only once in the many convoys I took where any sniper fire ever occurred. What surprised me was that the enemy didn't take the opportunity to ambush the convoys more often. They certainly seemed vulnerable to hit-and-run attacks.

Arriving at the battalion field position the trucks would disperse to their own company areas. I would set out for headquarters and find out the status of the companies. Sometimes the troops would be on a "stand-down" and I would find them all back in the battalion area. This would be very convenient for me since I could reach the entire battalion. At other times, I would discover that this or that company had been taken to work in another area of operation and would not be back for some time. I recall at times arriving at the field camp and being told the troops would be in that evening, I would fix my lean-to and foxhole only to find out later that an emergency situation had arisen and the battalion must be ready to move out in the hour. So I would hurriedly pack up, fill up the foxhole, dismantle the sleeping quarters and then give a hand to the troops. Many times I found myself moving heavy mortar ammo to the pick-up points.

When I arrived with the troops at the new location, things would be so bad from enemy contact that it was not feasible to have anything like a religious service. All I could do was simply spend the night there and make the best of a disappointing situation. The next morning it was necessary to leave and try to reach the next battalion on the schedule. So, packing up my gear and trudging up to a Chinook or hopping a truck, I would return to the supply trains at the airfield and hope that the next battalion on my list wouldn't be as tied up as the previous one. By this time I was grimier than ever. Before me is the prospect of another convoy ride out to the field. On the way there, a heavy rain drenches me and my vehicle is caught in the slime. Everyone piles out to help move it. The rain soon stops, and the mud cakes my face from the hot sun that is once again beating down.

I arrive at this battalion field area and go through the routine again of finding who is in and who is out. I am told that it will be late by the time three of the companies return. It is suggested I go out to an isolated company on the river. A Huey helicopter will be dropping off food and supplies to them and I might be able to hitch a ride. I cross my fingers when the Huey arrives and find they can take me. I am told I will have to stay with that company for the night since the copter won't return there until sometime the next morning. I could then return to the battalion area and from there take a convoy back to the airfield.

The Huey soon puts me down with the supplies at the company position on the river. I see I am actually on the river's edge and the ground is slimy and smells awful. Insects are swarming all around. If I am lucky I will find some boards on which I can later sleep. However, if the company has just arrived, there will not be any convenience like that and I will have to settle for sleeping in the muck. The one worthwhile part of this trip is that I am able to have a service for the troops. The looks in their faces show wonder that I should bother to come out to them in such a place as this. As I look over the small perimeter, and hear the strange sounds of tropical birds making their calls in the thick undergrowth, I feel isolated. This company of troops is very much on its own. What kind of night will this company have? Not being mechanized, their fire power is limited. It is doubtful they could hold off a heavy concerted attack. It would take time here before they could dig in with suitable defenses. I hope they will have the necessary time.

The next morning everyone looks more at ease. It was a quiet night. Then some firing is heard outside the perimeter. I find out that the ambush patrol which went out last night had itself been ambushed on its way in. The sounds of the firing are quickly over. Two of our men were killed just a little way from the perimeter. Their bodies are brought in. I see them. One had talked to me the night before. He had only a few weeks before returning to the States. Neither of us realized he would be returning home before then. The bodies are covered and a helicopter is called to remove them to graves registration. Mercifully for the living the copter is there quickly and the bodies are placed inside. As the copter goes off, a GI comes over to me with tears in his eyes. "We were like brothers, chaplain. Now I'm all alone." He walked away. Another GI came up a little later. "Please pray for me, chaplain. Please pray for me."

The Huey supply copter soon arrived and returned me to the battalion field area. I was then able to take the convoy back to the airfield. Arriving there I thanked the driver for the lift. Slinging my service kit on one shoulder and grabbing my gear I slowly made my way to another Wolfhound supply point. The friendly supply officer greeted me and had me place my gear in his tent. It felt wonderful to be sitting down in a real chair and resting for a few moments while getting information on what this battalion was doing and when its convoy would be leaving. It was almost noon and the captain invited me to go over with him to the mess tent and revitalize myself. I took him up on the offer and did feel better after some hot food.

In another hour we were on our way to the battalion field position. It was a rough trip and I was thankful I was in a jeep and not in a five ton truck. It was threatening rain. We soon arrived at the field position. Thanking the captain, I made my way to the command post and found that two companies were expected back soon and that two other companies had only a morning mission and were now back in camp resting for the night ambush patrol. I was a little surprised. "Did you say an entire company would be going out tonight?" The reply was affirmative. They would be taking up several different ambush positions during the course of the night. First they would move to point A, and after remaining there a while, they would move to point B, and so on. Since the enemy were doing a lot of moving at night, the high command decided to go after the enemy at night as well as look for them during the day. The hazards, of course, were increased for our troops. Not only were the possibilities of being ambushed in turn by the enemy greater, but there was also the added risk of being mistaken as enemy by your own planes as they flew around at night in search of troop movements. "Well, that's the chance they have to take," I was told.

In the evening, after having held services, I walked over to one of the companies preparing for the all night roving ambush. When words were spoken, you could detect anxiety in the tone of their voices. On went the harness belts, the grenades, the machine gun ammo. The darkness was such now that you had to go up to a person to recognize who he was. Watching these people prepare, I began to wonder what the pressures were on the troops in going out on this kind of mission. Moving out on a regular ambush was hard enough on the nerves, but once you arrived at a predetermined location, that was it. You prepared yourself for a long night with its attendant pressures. But what of the added pressures being repeated again and again in one night of moving now to this position and now to that position? Everytime you move, you are liable to being spotted, with the dire consequences of being ambushed yourself. The troops carrying out this mission have already been undergoing all sorts of pressures for many months. What added strain will this kind of mission bring to their already mentally and physically tired bodies? I decided to go out with them.

The company commander said he would be glad to have me along and that I would move with his group. The procedure was for three groups of soldiers to start out at ten minute intervals and proceed to a predetermined location where an ambush would then be set up. There they would remain for a given amount of time before moving off to another location. This procedure would continue throughout the night. It was hoped this tactic would enable our forces to make contact with the enemy.

The first group had been gone for about ten minutes when we received word to follow. As we left the perimeter I wondered if we would be around to see it the next morning. We were moving in single file. Off to the left along the horizon, you could see where flares were being dropped near Tan Son Nhut. For a while the faces of those near you were clear enough to be recognized. Then as the flares in the distance weakened in intensity, the faces again became impersonal dark masks. Even though the flares were at a great distance from us they still deprived us of our cover of darkness and you could feel the uneasiness of the troops as they would turn to look in the direction of a newly-dropped flare.

We were now a good distance from the battalion field area. Just before us was our first ambush position, an area surrounded by a hedgerow, rectangular in shape. The troops were positioned and we began to wait. Did anyone see us come into this hedgerow? If so, would they make any move against us while we were here? Or will they wait until we leave and are moving in single file before opening up on us? Or will some unsuspecting enemy move within range of our position? At this moment, our people are the hunters, but at what period this night will they become the hunted?

It was hard to believe that over an hour had passed. The commanding officer gave orders for the troops to prepare to move out to the next location. We were now crossing over some open fields. I noticed our troops walking over what appeared to be a large piece of cardboard. No one bothered to stop to examine it. The first group had already moved over this spot. I stopped and picked it up. There was a strange marking on it. Also it was torn in such a way as to present the form of a crude arrowhead. The captain studied it and recognized the markings as Chinese. This was a piece of cardboard from a Chinese K ration box. This cardboard was obviously being used as a sign to direct the

enemy troops along a specified night route. The captain immediately radioed the groups before and behind us about this, as
well as informing the base camp.

We soon reached our next ambush position, a cemetery. At
times the VC would hold fake funerals. Inside the coffins would
be weapons and ammunition which would be buried in a cemetery right under the eyes of authorities. At an appointed time,
they would come to the cemetery at night and dig up the arsenal. Before Tet there were an unusual number of funerals in
Saigon and elsewhere. So now we were waiting in a cemetery.
We were there for some time and soon I found myself fighting
off the desire to sleep with increasing difficulty. The temptation
to close your eyes and rest your head for just a moment is fierce.
You do not intend to go to sleep, you tell yourself. But you
know that if you give your body that moment, the chances are
you will doze right off. I began to roll my head back and forth,
looking intently into the darkness and hoping to see something
that would capture my attention. I started mumbling to myself,
"I must not sleep. I must not sleep." It was taking a tremendous
effort to keep awake. I started to move about. This helped, but
I remembered there are positions where you can't move at all,
and so I returned to my original place. Resisting sleep was so
hard. My eyelids were feeling heavier and heavier. How much
longer could I hold on? Then came the word, "Move out."

We were now moving along a canal. The ground was soft and
moist in texture. After a while our route changed in the direction of rice paddies. Our troops were using the berms to cross
over them, and so presented themselves as well defined targets.
It was clear the troops were tired. No longer were they bending
low to present as small a silhouette as possible. Now they were
moving upright and as I looked across at a nearby hedgerow the
thought occurred to me that if the enemy were in there, we were
in the position of clay ducks in a shooting gallery. No longer
were the troops looking to the right and left as they moved forward. Now their heads were cast down as they blindly followed

the man in front of them. Apparently they reached that state of fatigue in which you no longer have evaluative cognition, only conceptual. You are aware that you are moving about in a kind of darkness and that there are buddies in front and behind you, but the thought of the enemy no longer seemed significant.

We finally reached our next ambush position, a kind of triangular area overlooking a large plain. The troops were in position and it was not long before some snoring could be heard. The commanding officer, on hearing this, uttered some strong words and began to track down the tell-tale sound that indicated somebody was in dreamland. He found the GI and shocked him back to the present. It was clear why his buddies did not stop him. They too were out, only they were not snoring.

I returned with the commanding officer and as we looked out into the darkness he told me of an incident where in an ambush position everyone fell asleep. They had been going constantly for days with little or no sleep and then were sent out on an ambush at night. He recalled how he looked up to find three VC who passed through the perimeter and were staring down at him and two others beside him. It became apparent to the VC, when they sized up the situation that they were in the middle of a considerable number of Americans. One of them tried to remove a shotgun from the limp hands of one of the GI's, who sort of groaned and pulled it back. The VC then decided to leave. The captain said he didn't dare shoot, since the troops, being awakened with shots inside their perimeter, might turn around and there would develop a wild fire fight between the troops on one side of the square firing at the troops on the other side. So he waited till the VC had gotten out of the perimeter before doing any firing. By then it was too late and they escaped in the darkness.

There were several more moves that night. As the night wore on, and no VC or North Vietnamese were contacted, I began to realize how large this allegedly small country really was. It was no longer surprising to me that the North Vietnamese could move good-sized forces across the country at night and go undetected. With whole companies out looking for them they were difficult to find. While the Americans may have had over six hundred thousand troops in Vietnam, only about a tenth of these were combat troops. There were simply not enough of them to do the job effectively. And the few combat troops available were being overworked, rendering them even less effective.

Finally the dawn arrived. A signal flare was shot up into the sky to let those guarding the perimeter of the base camp know friendly troops were on their way in. About nine hours had elapsed. I thanked the commanding officer for permitting me to accompany his troops and then prepared to catch the morning convoy to the general supply area at the airfield. From there I would convoy to Cu Chi to make my hospital rounds, for it was Saturday already. The thought crossed my mind that tomorrow would then be Sunday and the field would again be my destination.

eighteen

It was late in May. I had arrived in the field with one of the Wolfhound units and had two services. The darkness was falling fast. From the moment of my arrival, I found myself involved with some of the troops on counseling matters about letters they had received from home. I never did find the opportunity to prepare a place for myself that night. With the rains making more and more frequent appearances, I always wanted to make sure to set the lean-to up, if at all possible. As it happened, I had nothing prepared and it was now dark. Since I felt tired, I decided to chance the rain and simply do without the rain cover. I walked about the area looking for a fairly flat place to sleep. Experience had taught me to check closely where you would be resting for the night. Being caught at the bottom of a natural gully or drainage flow was unconducive to a restful sleep during a downpour. I saw what looked perfect. The ground was flat and even clean. No ants were around either. You had to watch out for them; they were vicious. Going through hedgerows at times, a mass of ants might drop on you. You had to peel off your clothes quickly to get at those sadistic creatures before their metallic-like mandibles tore your flesh up. Next to the relentless pursuer the mosquito, the ant was among the cruelest of insects and far more a problem than even the scorpions who seemed curious about your flesh, but not voracious.

I decided on this area as the place I would rest for the night. I took the poncho-liner and put it on the ground. I was too tired even to blow up the air mattress. As I looked up at the night sky it dawned on me that there were no stars. "Must be very cloudy," I thought. "I bet it's going to rain tonight. If it does, then what?" I wanted to avoid getting wet if at all possible. Getting soaked at night with the chilly air made me miserable. As I looked about an idea came to me, "There's the place. Get under the truck. If it rains, you shouldn't get too wet." I started to get up. But I seemed somewhat comfortable where I was and so I decided to stay there. I kept turning and tossing. The thought of the rain returned again, and finally motivated me to get up and crawl under the truck. As I lay on my back, all I could now see was the underside of a rusting truck. I fell asleep.

I was awakened about a little after midnight by a sharp, ear-ringing metallic sound. I felt heat on one side of my face and could smell and taste what I was now familiar with— earth scorched by an explosive charge. At first I thought it was a mortar attack. I heard yelling. I looked about and then saw some GI's around the area where I had been earlier that night. I crawled out from under the truck and walked over to the spot. "What happened?" I asked. The battalion commander was also there and I heard someone call for a "Dust Off," the medic helicopter ship. The commanding officer told me that two of our troops were handling, against orders, the various weapons that our troops had captured that day from the enemy. One of the men accidentally triggered a loaded rocket launcher. The rocket landed twenty or so meters away and some of the shrapnel caught the two men. I looked at the hole in the ground. I saw the boot marks where I had been tossing and turning hours before over my decision to stay there or go over to the truck. The jagged aperture in the earth was about level with where my chest would have been. I mentioned to the commanding officer that I had been there originally, but later changed my mind in favor of sleeping under the truck. He replied in a matter-of-fact tone, "Padre, you would have been zapped for sure if you had stayed there," and turned around to check on the radio watch. I stared a while at the spot. I then looked up at the sky. There were stars now, shining very brightly.

Nothing else happened that night. The next morning I was making plans to move out to another Wolfhound battalion when word came over the radio from the battalion commander of the Mech that I come out to their field position immediately. I went back with the morning convoy to the airfield and from there hitched a ride on a convoy going to Cu Chi. At Cu Chi, I went to the Mech battalion headquarters to find out what means were available for me to get to the field. They informed me a Chinook would soon be leaving. I went over to my shelter and picked up my rifle. On occasions, I would take it along with the rest of my gear when I was advised the area I was going into was especially bad. Wally drove me to the Chinook pad and I was on my way.

When the Chinook reached the battalion area, I strained to see where they were. As we descended all that was visible was half a company of tracks. I left the Chinook and checked with one of the lieutenants who informed me the rest of the battalion had been ordered to a blocking position near an enemy troop route a few miles away. This group was to wait for certain materials from supply and then go meet the main force at that blocking point. I was told that the Mech had been hit on successive nights and had taken heavy casualties. A combat outpost was wiped out and the Mech had little to show for all the losses they were taking. The troops were in low spirits.

As we cautiously traveled over the terrain I was glad I brought the rifle along. The entire area had an atmosphere of hostility about it. I could sense it. The troops with me seemed unusually gloomy. It was evident that if the morale of the troops was low, then everyone would be in serious danger. To question your own confidence and ability in battle in time of imminent attack is bordering on suicide. The line between doing your job effectively and sheer paralysis in combat is thin. Our people had been going at it for some time. They were overworked and near exhaustion. Any further bad breaks might be disastrous.

When we arrived at the area where the battalion was to position themselves, we found they had arrived just moments before us. They had to go slowly to watch for mines. We had followed the route of their tracks and so moved faster. The position our battalion was ordered to take was right on one of the routes the enemy used in moving towards Saigon. Signs of carts and bikes used to transport weapons and ammo were clearly discernible from the markings on the ground. Whoever had the commanding officer take this position must have viewed it from the air where because of the foliage the terrain would not have looked as deeply inclined. But on the ground the position was like an oversize gully. As a result the tracks in the middle were forced to bunch together, offering multiple targets in a narrow area. It was already getting dark and there was no time to recon the area for possible adjustments in the original orders. The battalion commander was in a bind, since he was forced to move late in the day to an awkward position which would require time to properly fortify.

The faces of the men of the battalion showed they were under tremendous strain. I had never seen them looking so tired and haggard. The commanding officer told me what the situation was and asked if I would go around and speak with the troops.

I decided to go completely around the perimeter and see our troops. The terrain was rugged and thick. An ominous note was sounded when, as I began to make the rounds, an American helicopter off to our left was receiving machine gun fire from the enemy. The enemy were close by and there was no doubt they did not like having the Mech on their doorstep.

As I went around I recall commenting to the men on the tough going everyone was having recently. When they would mention our losses and seem overly despondent, I would jump on them about the fact that it was about time the Mech started being its old self, that they had been pushed around long enough. It was time to start getting mad. I told them I hoped the enemy did come that night, that I was sick of hearing what they were doing to us. "They've been sniping at you, placing booby traps and mines against you, mortaring you. Now, the enemy is getting brazen enough to come right up to you. It's about time we started to do something besides feeling sorry for ourselves."

I had soon covered the entire perimeter. It was dark. If ever the enemy had an opportunity, it was this night. With no time to properly prepare, our battalion was in a critical posture. If the enemy did attack, however, I felt convinced our men would fight like their old selves, despite their weariness and setbacks, but it would be costly. I realized I had been harsh at times in how I spoke to them. I felt bad about that. I loved them deeply. There was nothing more I wanted to do emotionally than openly sympathize with them in their complaints over their bad luck, but I could not enjoy the luxury of those emotions when their lives were in critical danger. In the darkness I closed my eyes and prayed for them.

It seemed to all of us like a miracle. The enemy did not strike during the night. They missed their big chance. With a new day before our troops, and time to properly set themselves up, you could feel a general atmosphere of renewed confidence. The little bit of time everyone needed to recuperate mentally and emotionally was granted. They were over the crisis. The battalion commanding officer suggested I hold a service. I did and was astonished at the number of troops that attended. The Mech never did set any records for attending any kind of religious services. Today it seemed as though the whole battalion was there. We had all been through something the night before. No doubt many of them attended simply because they wanted to let me know they appreciated my coming out to share that critical night with them. But I would rather think it was perhaps the beginning of a long and deeper relationship with God, no matter how they may express it in the future, through formal or informal religion.

During the rest of the day the battalion made its preparations well and that night they were ready. Nothing occurred that night either. It was the third day now, and I knew I still had another battalion to reach a good distance away. I packed up my gear and went for the Chinook point. As I passed my battalion commander, I gave him a friendly salute, and he responded with a warm smile as well. I thought to myself, "I wish we had more battalion commanders like that one."

I was later to find out that that night the enemy did launch a ground attack against the Mech with flame throwers, but the Mech was ready, and the enemy again knew them as the "Bobcats."

nineteen

It was now the beginning of June. In about three months my tour in Vietnam would be over. I did not, however, give any thought to getting "short." I had seen too many instances of men with only a few days to go having tragedy befall their loved ones on the news of their death.

With only a few months remaining, my friends were pressuring me to take my R&R, Rest and Recuperation. The government would fly you free to certain localities where you could stay for a period extending up to seven days. You had a choice of Singapore, Hong Kong, Taiwan, Bangkok, Australia, Panang or Hawaii. For the troops in Vietnam to qualify for the R&R, they normally had to have six months of their tour completed. One R&R was allotted for a given tour, although there were those who obtained more. While there were certain intrinsic aspects of R&R that were commendable, there were other characteristics of the program that tarnished the overall picture.

I remember reading a brochure on R&R put out by the service. It gave a general description of each R&R center and how you would go about choosing a girl companion during your visit. I still remember GI's showing me pictures of the girls they lived with during their R&R. There was one young lady in Bangkok whose picture kept appearing in quite a few different wallets. No doubt, even if a GI didn't sleep with a companion he would still come back with romantic stories so as not to have others regard him as some kind of misfit for not getting all he could of the pleasures of life. When many of the GI's returned from their R&R, their buddies would lay bets on when they would have to start visiting the "Doc" for the necessary shots. Many of the doctors told me, however, that there was far greater danger of the troops catching a serious disease from the Boom Boom girls who frequented the perimeter areas in Nam than from the R&R areas. However true that may be, the danger was still there. The point I am making is that the service seemed to be contradicting itself: there was its general policy warning against venereal disease and then there was this R&R brochure seemingly encouraging them to place themselves in a situation where the risk of this disease was possible.

Along with this personal risk to the GI was the image of America being given the rest of the world. The image of the "Ugly American" is bad enough without adding to it ludicrousness by its exaggeration of sex, as manifested in the frantic acclaim and wild clamor of troops at a performance by some female dancer. Their reactions seemed "unreal, unnatural, excessive, overdone," according to some Vietnamese. Another said that if that reaction was representative of Americans in general, then they must be "sex-obsessed barbarians."

Whether the Vietnamese I talked with really believed this, I do not know, but I did detect a certain bitterness in their expressions. Perhaps what was really bothering the Vietnamese male was that these non-yellow foreigners were coming into his country, ostensibly to help him against a common enemy, while in fact they were humiliating the Vietnamese male by taking away his women. I used to remind the troops in the field that an added reason for refraining from playing around with the Vietnamese women was to lessen the reason for the VC and North Vietnamese to fight with such stubbornness. It is one thing to fight for some political principle and another to fight to vindicate your manhood. I feel that many of the Vietnamese people our troops fought came to develop a deeper and more personal hatred over the relationship many of our men were having with their women than over political reasons. I recall many an argument with certain American officers who condoned the sexual activities of the troops. They argued the troops needed to "relax." In my opinion our troops were losing in the beds what was being won on the battlefields. There is a time for work and a time for play. But if your playing works ultimately against your best interests, then such play may be likened to the "rapture of the depths." Intoxicating and wonderful, although it is killing you.

As for myself, I never did take an R&R. To me R&R was like crumbs being given by my government to our troops as compensation for making them expendable in a game of politics. I would have preferred my government doing more to protect our troops from being unnecessarily killed by the enemy. Taking more meaningful steps to lessen the enemy being so well supplied would have been better than taking steps to see that the troops were entertained for a week in Bangkok. Many a GI would return from his R&R and shortly after get killed. We may paraphrase here an earlier statement: "The condemned also had a hearty R&R."

twenty

When I arrived at one of the Wolfhound battalions, the commanding officer asked that a memorial service be held for those men of the battalion who had lost their lives in the past month. Usually the memorial service was delayed until the battalion returned to Cu Chi, thus affording time for a more formal ceremony.

The memorial service was always grim. The names of the men who had lost their lives were read aloud followed by a moment of prayerful silence to show respect and honor to their memory. After the general memorial service, there would often be private religious services for any troops who wished to attend.

If the memorial service was held in Cu Chi, the ceremony was more elaborate and emotionally trying. There the troops would line up in strict order, forming a square. The commanding officer would speak and then the chaplain, after the military band had presented appropriate music. The names of the dead were called out, and at each name a GI would come forward to a designated position, invert the rifle he was carrying with fixed bayonet, and plunge it into the ground. Then he would take off his helmet and place it on the rifle stock. Stepping back he would salute and return to his place in the ranks. By the time the list reached the final name, there would be a disheartening number of rifles piercing the ground. It was an eerie experience to look upon those silent, inverted weapons with helmets resting inert upon them. Taps would then sound, followed by several moments of silence. After this the ceremony ended.

Many of the troops told me they found such ceremonies trying, since memories were brought back of their friends in a way that reopened the wounds of loss. I suspect the reason the commanding officer preferred holding the memorial service in the field, whenever possible, was to try and lighten this painful experience.

By the time the memorial services were over it was dark and the troops settled down to the work at hand. The ambush units would soon be sent out. I hoped they would not have the problem that some other units had from another battalion when one group left ahead of the other. When the second ambush unit left the base camp, they went in the wrong direction and walked into the area of the first unit who by this time were set up. The first unit, thinking these people the enemy, opened fire. Both units then called in that they had made contact. When the second unit gave the map coordinates of where the enemy fire was coming from and requested artillery support, headquarters looked at the map and found this was exactly the position where the first ambush unit was supposed to be. Both units were told to hold their fire. Each did and was surprised to find that the firing had also stopped from the side of the presumed enemy. Amazingly enough no one was injured on either side. A tragedy was averted since the artillery would have had no trouble in reaching its target.

No such problem developed this night. All was quiet. Since the battalion area included a small cemetery, I chose a place to sleep where a cement border surrounded a grave and its tombstone. Being ever so slightly off the slimy damp ground was a luxury. I set up my poncho so as to give me some protection from the rain. However, I neglected to tighten sufficiently the single place where rain could reach me, through the hood portion of the poncho. Around midnight a heavy rain fell. The relentlessly probing rain soon discovered the susceptible part of my poncho and before long I noticed an ominous bulge just over my face. The weight of the water was increasing in the hood and breakthrough was imminent. I hoped the rain would stop before the inevitable happened. I had no such luck. The warmth I was enjoying from the rainy dampness was soon lost as the cold water gushed over me. "Well," I thought, "the ambush units are in a far more uncomfortable predicament. At least I am inside the perimeter on a cement slab instead of outside the wire in a rain-filled ditch."

After a while the rain stopped and for several hours it was clear and quiet. Then mortars began falling into the battalion area. They seemed to be dropping helter-skelter. No walk-in pattern as I experienced shortly before with another battalion, where I heard the hollow-sounding "thump, thump, thump" of the mortar tubes, followed shortly by the sharp, metallic, crunching sound of the mortars landing. There, too, I had no overhead cover and was on ground level, but there the enemy was walking the mortars in a definite line. With every discharge and subsequent adjustment of their tubes, they were moving closer and closer to our position. It was obvious that with one more adjustment they would have their mortars landing right on our heads. By this time, however, our own mortar crews had the enemy flashes spotted and began counter-mortar fire. This discouraged the enemy and their firing ceased. In tonight's mortar attack our crews were slow in responding and for an excruciating length of time the enemy's mortars were dropping in all over the place. The voice of the operations officer could be heard for some distance as he screamed orders to the mortar units to get off their duff and start firing. His voice was getting louder by the second. Not to reply to the enemy immediately when they shot at you was inviting trouble. Finally the mortar teams were able to return fire and the enemy tubes soon were quiet. Several of our people were wounded and one was killed as a result of that attack. Considering the number of rounds that came into the area for so long most of the battalion was fortunate.

The next morning I returned to the general supply area and was invited by a battalion supply officer to go with him to have a steam bath. I had often heard that Tan Son Nhut had some of these places and had often dreamed of being able to utilize such a facility to remove the accumulated grime of almost ten months. Since the next convoy would not be leaving for several hours I decided to take him up on his offer.

When the jeep stopped I noticed that the building we were to enter had no signs about steam baths. The place turned out to be a bar. "Where's the steam bath?" I asked my friend. "We'll get to that later. It's hot. Let's have a drink," he replied. It was evident he had been in this place before. Everybody, including the bar girls, knew him. One of them came up to me and said, "Buy me a drink, honey?" I knew that she meant "Saigon Tea" which was supposed to be a shot of hard liquor at hard liquor prices but was actually colored water. This was one way the girls in the bars made their living. The other way was by prostitution. By now my captain friend was enjoying himself with one of the other girls. The girl that came over to me was giving a "number one" sell with samplings. I did not want to hurt nor embarrass her. Yet, I had to make it clear to her that I did not want to become involved in what she had in mind. I pointed in the direction of my grimy collar to the cross insignia, designating me a Christian chaplain. Jewish chaplains would wear the tablets insignia on their collar. I used the Vietnamese word, "Cha," meaning "Father." She looked closely at the insignia and then again at me. She slowly moved back, and her face was deeply apologetic. "You are a priest?" she said, "I am sorry . . . I did not know."

At that point a seedy-looking bartender came up and said rather roughly to her, "Another drink?" It was her job to down the "Saigon Tea" shots in quick order so that the American's bill would be sky high by the time he left the bar. I recall a GI telling me he spent over eighty dollars in a Saigon bar on drinks for the girl alone. So when the young lady I was with told the bartender "No more" and to stay away, he looked at her with surprise and anger. She then told me something about herself. Her father was killed in the war and she was supporting her mother and younger brothers and sisters in this way. She was ashamed of what she was doing but she knew of no other way to make so much needed money. She then apologized again and said goodbye. She went over to sit at a table with some of the other girls waiting for GI's to enter the bar. The captain who brought me there saw this and decided to call it a day. "Guess we might as well be going," he said. I agreed. When we were outside and going to the jeep I asked, "What about the steam bath?" He mentioned that it was getting late, and that we had best return to the supply area. "Well," I resignedly thought to myself, "perhaps this is what he meant by the 'steam bath' all along." In that context, he was certainly right.

The captain dropped me off at the convoy point and I hopped into a truck which would be going in the direction of Cu Chi. I was told a company of the "Hounds" was guarding the Hoc Mon bridge and so I decided to try to hold a service for them. As we approached the bridge I gave a prearranged signal to the driver who slowed down enough for me to get off. The commanding officer of the company told me I could have the service later in the day. While waiting I walked around the bridge defenses. Because a river canal was there, the area the troops had to work was soft and slimy. If you slipped off the walks leading to the various bunker positions you ended up filthy with a stench on you that made the aroma of the water buffalo smell like expensive perfume.

The time for the service arrived and I saw that it would have to be held alongside the road since there wasn't any other place available. Much grime and dust was coming off the road on us, while the cacophonous noise of the traffic just a few feet away, along with the jabbering of the passing Vietnamese, shattered any chance of the calm quiet we would have liked. Yet the troops did not seem to mind at all. They were used to living with inconveniences and were not distracted from the things they considered important.

After the service I spoke with some of the troops. Later the commanding officer informed me that there would be no more convoys passing through. That meant I would be spending the night at the bridge. I had intended to sleep alongside the road but the number of massive rats I saw running about at night drove me to sleep on the bridge itself, although this was an important target to the enemy and I would have preferred not being on it, especially at night. It turned out to be a quiet night. I even slept for a couple of hours!

The next day I caught a mail run on its way to Cu Chi and arrived there in time to begin the weekly hospital rounds. It was then I received some surprising news. I was being transferred from my job as an infantry chaplain to division artillery. With less than two months to complete my tour, this seemed strange. I was told that the present brigade chaplain, a major, was completing his tour, and the major replacing him happened to be Catholic. In a brigade, the allotment is one Catholic and three non-Catholic chaplains. With the new brigade chaplain Catholic, I would have to go as a Catholic chaplain. It was decided, however, there was no need for me to have to leave the 25th Division altogether, since there was an opening in division artillery for a Catholic chaplain. I noted that one of the non-Catholic chaplains in a battalion had just made the rank of major. Why not have him take the brigade chaplain's slot? Then I could remain. However, it was determined he would take the brigade chaplain slot in Support Command.

I have always wondered if someone had reported my being in combat gear. As mentioned earlier, the chaplain's office was sensitive to its members carrying weapons. "Well," I thought, "we have seen something of Support Command and a great deal of the infantry. It looks like we're now going to have the chance to find out how the artillery operates."

Leaving the infantry, however, was not easy for me. I had grown to know and love them. The thought of not having Wally any longer as my assistant made the transfer even more difficult. A good and loyal assistant is hard to come by. I would greatly miss all of them.

twenty-one

The remaining time of my tour in Vietnam went by quickly. The routine I found at division artillery (DIVARTY) was different to what I was accustomed to. First, I was no longer traveling alone but with another chaplain. We would go together each day to different field batteries and hold services for the troops there. No longer did I have to be mauled in a truck convoy, or wait long hours in the sun for a noisy Chinook. DIVARTY had its own helicopters and we received what was almost a private taxi service. When the helicopters were flying out to an assigned mission they would take us along and leave us at some battery on the way. When the copters were released from their assigned task they would pick us up on their return. In this way we were able to hold two and sometimes even three services in one day.

Another advantage of DIVARTY was that their personnel would be at their field positions when you arrived because of their tactical function. Only if they had to "redball" to some area would they not be there and we were usually warned about that. In a "redball," the artillery personnel take their guns and ride off to a temporary location where they do their firing and then return to their original battery position. With the luxury of immediately accessible transportation, along with the assured presence of the troops when you arrived at their field positions, I found that by the end of any given week, my number of services held in the field had tripled. The bulk of my time was no longer used trying to reach the troops.

My new living conditions were also remarkably changed. I did not have to live out in the field five or so days each week. Each night I would be back at Cu Chi. The bunker I shared with several other officers was actually an underground living quarters. The bunk had a mattress with sheets and a pillow. By sleeping there at night, you could rest more securely from rocket and mortar attacks. The officers even had a television set in the bunker. This was not all. There were three hot meals a day, at regular hours, served to you in a room with furniture and silverware. I felt as though I had emerged from the tomb.

Something that I especially noticed about the artillery was their attempt to make field life as livable as possible. It is true that their relatively static position in the field gave them certain advantages the infantry simply could not have, but I noticed that in such matters as latrines the artillery were far more adept, especially concerning privacy. The name "grunt" or "crunchy" comes close to describing how near to the earth the infantry soldier must live. However, it seemed the infantry went out of its way to stress its earthiness. The longer a man is out in the field, the more animal and the less rational he becomes. Stressing man's animal side did not seem to be good psychologically. Despite living in inhuman situations, it is necessary for the ground soldier to keep reminding himself that he is more than an animal. He is a human being and winning the battle will be a Pyrrhic victory if in doing so he has lost his sense of being human. The subject of field latrines may seem to be trivial, but when a man is in the field he has little and the apparently little things can prove to be significant in the overall formation that is taking place within this man.

twenty-two

It was the middle of August. While the situation around Saigon was under control, the enemy were now active about Tay Ninh and Dau Tieng. It was reported that my friends in the 5th Mech took a pounding from the enemy in that area and the casualty list was growing. While visiting the hospital one day, I came upon Lt. Snodgras, who had recently taken over a company in the Mech. The lieutenant described to me the bad times up there, especially in the Michelin rubber plantation. There, in a recent fire fight, he had sustained serious injuries to his shoulder and arm. I asked if there was anything I could get him. He mentioned that his cigarette lighter was lost during the turmoil of the fire fight and requested some matches. I could see he would have difficulty lighting anything with his incapacitated right arm and so I asked if he would accept the cigarette lighter which a group of the officers in the Mech presented to me when I left for my new assignment with DIVARTY. Although I didn't smoke, I personally treasured that lighter, along with the plaque which had on it a replica of the badge of the combat infantryman. Coming from those men who knew so well the hardships of combat, such a gift was priceless to me. While I would never give up that plaque, it seemed this was a situation which warranted my giving up the "Bobcat" lighter. Here was a fellow "Bobcat" who needed it. I mentioned to him that the lighter had my name on it. Would that be all right? He graciously accepted it as a parting remembrance of our friendship.

When I returned that morning from the hospital, I was informed by the senior chaplain that Col. Sumner, the commanding officer, wanted the chaplains to go to a battery near Tay Ninh where the troops had undergone a ground attack the night before and suffered serious casualties. When we arrived there, the look in the faces of the artillery troops was familiar. Firing your big guns at an enemy some distance away is one thing, but having the enemy right on you and seeing his face is quite another. The troops had handled themselves well, but they were none the less shaken up. Services were held for the troops and they seemed to appreciate our presence.

This was but the beginning of many such experiences for a number of the artillery batteries stationed around these areas. I recall speaking later with troops of some other batteries who also had harrowing experiences with the enemy ground attacks. One "Redleg" told me of seeing his lieutenant struck by an RPG rocket, which splattered parts of his body over the gun block. Action was more and more frequent and the pressure was now growing on the artillery troops. They were feeling that sense of imminent danger so familiar to the infantry.

During these periods of pressure there would be certain musical songs played over the Armed Forces Radio, which especially appealed to the combat soldier. One song which dug to the innards of the soldiers was "San Francisco." Every time a jet was seen in the sky, someone would yell, "Freedom Bird!" and the theme of that song would then come to mind. "San Francisco" was symbolic of home. "Little Green Apples" was also popular, perhaps because of the familiar memories it stimulated which were in such contrast to the present situation. Another song which seemed to capture the atmosphere of the soldier's condition was "Master Jack." The words of that song were strangely applicable to the thoughts of a soldier who would rather be elsewhere than on this foreign soil, thousands of miles away from home and awaiting the inevitable, with darkness now swiftly enshrouding him in an atmosphere that breathed ever more heavily of the oncoming presence of the enemy.

twenty-three

The helicopter approached the landing pad near the replacement depot in Long Binh. It seemed hard to believe a year had gone by. I was but a few hours from boarding that "Freedom Bird." While descending in the copter I looked to see if there were any major changes since I arrived a year ago. There seemed to be more sandbags on the long ground level bunkers for protection against mortars, but certainly of no value if hit by a 122 rocket.

When the copter landed I bade farewell to the young pilot, who had just recently come to Vietnam. Those copter pilots were in a class by themselves. How they could handle their ships! They could maneuver with great precision, skimming the ground by a few feet, and then at the last moment bounding over the hedgerows or buildings and again going low to the ground. This was not all for the fun of it. Often such flying was necessary to lessen the chances of being an easy target for enemy gunfire. Either you had to be quite high or very low. To be anywhere in the middle was suicide. The copter pilots I knew did a remarkable job of flying.

As the copter rose up and went on its way I stood at the pad for a long time, watching it slowly fade away in the direction of Cu Chi. The many times I had flown with the different pilots raced across my mind—Mark, Lt. Bob, "Pooch," the "captain," "Hotrod" and others, all under the paternal tutelage of "Big Daddy." They were a wonderful group. I remember especially Mark, who was never simply satisfied with flying to a given destination but always kept scanning the area below for any sign of enemy movement. If anything looked suspicious, he would call it in and then go down to take a closer look. Later, when I was back in "the world," Mark would write me to tell me that he had received the Silver Star. I was not at all surprised, knowing the kind of person I had been flying with. Still later, I would receive the terrible news that Mark had been killed in action.

The copter was gone now. I turned away from the landing pad and slowly made my way to the administration building and signed in. Milling around were a number of other officers awaiting their flight time, as well as the new arrivals awaiting transportation to their assignments in the various corps areas of Vietnam. We were given a briefing on departure proceedings, and then directed to exchange our scrip for U.S. currency. We rented the bed linens for our bunk (I was delighted to see that the price had not gone up!) and waited for the flight departure time which was supposed to be tomorrow at 1500 hours. Leaving at three in the afternoon was ideal. First, because travel in the bus would be in daylight. Second, the chances of any kind of attack, mortar or otherwise, was slight. The barracks assigned me was crowded and the only available bunk was an upper. This was not a good place to be should mortars happen to come in.

Except for the occasional report from the guns of some far off battery giving harassing fire against the enemy things were quiet that night. Actually the situation around Long Binh was tame compared to Cu Chi or the field. However, with the advent of the 122 rocket, one could never feel secure.

The next morning I received the news that my original flight was delayed until 0200 hours the following morning. For some reason, this did not surprise me. Leaving comfortably at three in the afternoon simply did not fit the general pattern of my Vietnam tour. To have to leave at two in the morning was really more like it. Besides, that was rocket time at the Bien Hoa airfield. That delay would also mean another night at the replacement center which was like limbo: you were neither here nor there.

Midnight, the designated time to leave the replacement center for the airfield, finally arrived. We were herded into a bus which resembled the one I boarded a year ago. The metal screens were still on the windows. As the bus pulled away I noticed that our only security was a jeep up ahead. None of us had any weapons. To be traveling on the road at night in this kind of situation made me uncomfortable. It would be so easy for someone to fire off one rocket and then disappear in the darkness. There was an apprehensive silence within the bus. Finally we reached the Bien Hoa airfield. We were taken to the large terminal area where a year ago we first came after leaving the plane. The place now had substantial looking bunkers in case of rocket attacks. We sat on some wooden benches waiting for our plane. It was approaching 0200 hours. Would this be one of the nights Charlie would be playing with his rockets? Then came the heavy drone of a jet landing. It was our plane. A crowd of about two hundred let out a loud yell of approval. Their plane was here. Then came the moment I had wondered about a year ago: "What do you look like when you have just come from the States and have landed at Bien Hoa, your first moments in Vietnam?" I remembered the crowd which a year ago greeted our group that had just landed. Now I found myself with a similar crowd that was returning to the States. The arrivals soon appeared. The crowd I was with howled with delight. I remained silent. I was seeing myself of one year ago and saw no reason to howl.

After the arrivals were off the plane, we were told to board it immediately. There was always the possibility of Charlie throwing in some rockets, hoping for a lucky hit on a ship that was to fly the GI's home after their year in Vietnam. To strike such a ship somewhere on its take-off would be a real demoralizer to those other GI's looking forward to their own departure date. And so we were ordered to run to the plane. And there I was with the rest of them, running to the plane. A year ago when I had arrived I walked off the plane. Now a year later we were told to run to the plane to get away. Is this all that was accomplished in the whole year? After facing up to the enemy all year—your last moment in Vietnam, forever remembered, was that you were told to run to the plane to get away. Every step became heavier and heavier. An intense feeling of frustration and disgust was coursing through my body. I wanted to walk. I did not want to run. I wanted to leave Vietnam with honor, not a sense of shame. But there were two hundred other men on this flight and their welfare came before one's insulted sense of honor. And so I ran.

When I arrived at the plane the officers were to board up front, enlisted men in the rear. Maybe they would have me run, but by God they were not going to tell me where I should sit. I chose to sit with the enlisted men—the reason I came to Vietnam in the first place. Inside the plane I located a seat near the galley section. The soldier next to me was a combat type. The group I found myself with turned out to be all infantrymen. I felt at home.

The plane was a Douglas DC-8 and belonged to the Flying Tiger Line. I must admit I was not pleased when I first heard my flight back would be on that line. In my ignorance I contemplated some old crate that had transported war material over the "hump" in the Second World War. I envisaged a decrepit pilot in a wheelchair coming out to fly the heap. This was a pleasant surprise. As the ship started off for the take-off a still hush pervaded within. Then came that moment of lift-off. Someone yelled excitedly, "Go, Freedom Bird, go!" And so it did, farther and farther away from Vietnam, amid wild shouts of exhilaration among the troops.

The pilot welcomed us aboard and told us to relax. The stewardesses started to prepare the first of many meals. As I sat back I began to think about what was happening. All of us on this plane were on our way home. I repeated it several times, but found that I was filled with mixed emotions. There was a certain joy in my heart that the nightmare was over for me. But then, that was the point. It may have been over for me, but it was not over for so many others still there. How could I be happy, when my friends were still there? I looked at my watch. It was about two thirty in the morning, a dangerous time for those boys in the field; a lonely, fearful time for the boys on ambush; an agonizing time for those seriously wounded and in the intensive care ward at the 12th Evac Hospital, and hospitals like it all over the corps area. In a few hours, it will be daylight there. The boys, still shivering from the chilly rains, will then have another day to be scorched by the sun, bitten by insects, and revolted by the leeches that will be drawing their blood when they ford the canals. They will be wondering who will get the job of point man this day, and whether there will be many booby traps in the areas they must enter. How can I be happy when some of those young men who are now alive will be dead before this day is out, others perhaps without their limbs, their arms or their sight? I had come to Vietnam in apprehension, but with hope. I find I left it in disappointment and with sorrow.

about the author

J. Robert Falabella was born in Philadelphia, Pennsylvania, in 1930. Upon completion of studies at Gonzaga High School, he was awarded the Civitan Honor Key. His studies focused on Greek, Latin, philosophy, biology, and computer programming, all of which he taught for several years. He went on to receive bachelor and licentiate degrees in theology at Woodstock, Maryland, where he was ordained to the priesthood in 1961. After a few more years of teaching theology, he volunteered to be an Army chaplain in Vietnam from 1967 to 1968 with the 25th Infantry Division; he was awarded the Army Commendation Medal, the Silver Star, the Bronze Star, and the Certificate of Achievement. Completing his three-year military commitment, he continued his priestly work and cared for a pontifical institute of Religious Sisters for ten years, and for the last six years he has been a priest in residence at St. Mary Magdalene Catholic Church in Simpsonville, South Carolina.

The Naval Institute Press is the book-publishing arm of the U.S. Naval Institute, a private, nonprofit, membership society for sea service professionals and others who share an interest in naval and maritime affairs. Established in 1873 at the U.S. Naval Academy in Annapolis, Maryland, where its offices remain today, the Naval Institute has members worldwide.

Members of the Naval Institute support the education programs of the society and receive the influential monthly magazine *Proceedings* or the colorful bimonthly magazine *Naval History* and discounts on fine nautical prints and on ship and aircraft photos. They also have access to the transcripts of the Institute's Oral History Program and get discounted admission to any of the Institute-sponsored seminars offered around the country.

The Naval Institute's book-publishing program, begun in 1898 with basic guides to naval practices, has broadened its scope to include books of more general interest. Now the Naval Institute Press publishes about seventy titles each year, ranging from how-to books on boating and navigation to battle histories, biographies, ship and aircraft guides, and novels. Institute members receive significant discounts on the Press's more than eight hundred books in print.

Full-time students are eligible for special half-price membership rates. Life memberships are also available.

For a free catalog describing Naval Institute Press books currently available, and for further information about joining the U.S. Naval Institute, please write to:

Member Services
U.S. Naval Institute
291 Wood Road
Annapolis, MD 21402-5034
Telephone: (800) 233-8764
Fax: (410) 571-1703
Web address: www.usni.org